# PRAYING
## WITH
## ANCIENT
## ISRAEL

### EXPLORING THE THEOLOGY OF PRAYER
### IN THE OLD TESTAMENT

D1563408

### EDITED BY

## PHILLIP G. CAMP AND TREMPER LONGMAN III

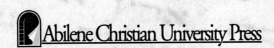

Abilene Christian University Press

# PRAISE FOR PRAYING WITH ANCIENT ISRAEL

"Designed to be comprehensive and accessible, this volume explores both the diversity and vitality of prayer in the Old Testament. It will prove to be an important theological resource for students, pastors, and scholars."

—William P. Brown,
*William Marcellus McPheeters Professor*
*of Old Testament at Columbia Theological Seminary*

"It is clear that when we pray, we stand in a long line of those who have prayed. We do not invent the cadences and habits of prayer, but rather we echo and reiterate the faithfulness of those who have preceded us. The book will serve both as a welcome exposition of scripture and as instruction to our own work of prayer."

—Walter Brueggemann,
*professor Emeritus, Columbia Theological Seminary*

"Close reading of how and why Israel prayed, as this book ably demonstrates, deepens our understanding of the nature, character, and purposes of God, and by extension, of the promise and potential of the Church at prayer in and for the world. For communities of faith, such a book will no doubt be more than an important addition to the library; it will be a generative resource for robust participation in the ongoing discourse between heaven and earth."

—Samuel Balentine,
*professor of Old Testament, Union Presbyterian Seminary*

"The new starting point for the study of prayer in the Hebrew Bible. In dialogue with recent research, this volume exposes readers to the rich and diverse canonical traditions of prayer. Wise contributions, accessibly written."

—Mark J. Boda,
*Professor of Old Testament, McMaster Divinity College;*
*professor, Faculty of Theology, McMaster University*

# Praying with Ancient Israel
## Exploring the Theology of Prayer in the Old Testament

Copyright © 2015 by Edited by Phillip G. Camp and Tremper Longman III

ISBN 978-089112-379-8

Printed in the United States of America

ALL RIGHTS RESERVED

No part of this publication may be reproduced, stored in a retrieval system, or transmitted in any form by any means—electronic, mechanical, photocopying, recording, or otherwise—without prior written consent.

Scripture quotations noted ESV are from The ESV® Bible (The Holy Bible, English Standard Version®) copyright © 2001 by Crossway, a publishing ministry of Good News Publishers ESV ® Text Edition: 2011. The ESV® text has been reproduced in cooperation with and by permission of Good News Publishers. Unauthorized reproduction of this publication is prohibited. All rights reserved.

Quotations marked NETS are taken from A New English Translation of the Septuagint, ©2007 by the International Organization for Septuagint and Cognate Studies, Inc. Used by permission of Oxford University Press. All rights reserved.

Scripture quotations marked NIV are taken from The Holy Bible, New International Version®, NIV®. Copyright © 1973, 1978, 1984, 2011 by Biblica, Inc.® Used by permission. All rights reserved worldwide.

Scripture quotations noted NRSV are taken from the New Revised Standard Version Bible, copyright © 1989, the Division of Christian Education of the National Council of the Churches of Christ in the United States of America. Used by permission. All rights reserved.

Cover design by Marc Whitaker

Interior text design by Becky Hawley

For information contact:
Abilene Christian University Press
ACU Box 29138
Abilene, Texas 79699
1-877-816-4455
www.acupressbooks.com

14 15 16 17 18 19 / 7 6 5 4 3 2 1

# TABLE OF CONTENTS

# ACKNOWLEDGEMENTS

The chapters presented in this volume, with one exception, were originally presented as papers over three years at the Thomas H. Olbricht Christian Scholars' Conference (2012, 2013, and 2014) at Lipscomb University in Nashville, Tennessee. We are grateful to the conference coordinator, David Fleer, for including our session on the theology of prayer in the Old Testament in the program each of those years, and we appreciate the feedback from those who attended the sessions at those conferences.

I (Phillip Camp) also want to thank Lipscomb University for a summer writing grant in 2014 that allowed me to complete my contributions to the book and begin the editing process. I am grateful to my colleagues in the Hazelip School of Theology at Lipscomb University for their feedback on my chapter on prayer in the Pentateuch.

Finally, we are grateful to Abilene Christian University Press for publishing this volume and especially to Mary Hardegree and Jason Fikes for their advice and guidance as we moved through the process.

Phillip G. Camp
Tremper Longman III

# ABBREVIATIONS

| | |
|---|---|
| AB | Anchor Bible |
| AOTC | Apollos Old Testament Commentary |
| ASV | American Standard Version |
| *BBR* | *Bulletin for Biblical Research* |
| BCOT | Baker Commentary on the Old Testament |
| BDB | Brown, Francis, S. R. Driver, and Charles A. Briggs, *A Hebrew and English Lexicon of the Old Testament*. Oxford: Claredon Press, 1907. |
| BETL | Bibliotheca ephemeridum theologicarum lovaniensium |
| BibSem | The Biblical Seminar |
| *BSac* | *Bibliotheca Sacra* |
| BZAW | Beihefte zur Zietschrift für die alttestamentliche Wissenschaft |
| *CBQ* | *Catholic Biblical Quarterly* |
| CC | Continental Commentary |
| EBC | The Expositor's Bible Commentary |
| ESV | English Standard Version |
| *EvQ* | *Evangelical Quarterly* |
| FAT | Forschungen Zum Alten Testament |
| *HBT* | *Horizons in Biblical Theology* |
| *HCBD* | *Harper Collins Bible Dictionary* |
| *HALOT* | *The Hebrew and Aramaic Lexicon of the Old Testament.* |
| HCSB | Holman Christian Standard Bible |
| IBC | Interpretation: A Bible Commentary for Teaching and Preaching |

| | |
|---|---|
| IDB | Interpreter's Dictionary of the Bible |
| *JAOS* | *Journal of the American Oriental Society* |
| *JBL* | *Journal of Biblical Literature* |
| *JETS* | *Journal of the Evangelical Theological Society* |
| JPSBC | Jewish Publication Society Bible Commentary |
| JPSTC | Jewish Publication Society Torah Commentary |
| *JSOT* | *Journal for the Study of the Old Testament* |
| JSOTSup | Journal for the Study of the Old Testament: Supplement Series |
| *JSS* | *Journal of Semitic Studies* |
| KJV | King James Version |
| *LS* | *Louvvain Studies* |
| LXX | Septuagint |
| MT | Masoretic Text |
| NAC | New American Commentary |
| NASB | New American Standard Bible |
| NCB | New Century Bible |
| NETS | New English Translation of the Septuagint |
| NIB | New Interpreter's Bible |
| NIBC | New International Biblical Commentary |
| NICOT | New International Commentary on the Old Testament |
| NIV | New International Version |
| NJB | New Jerusalem Bible |
| NJPS | *Tanakh: The Holy Scriptures: The New JPS Translation according to the Traditional Hebrew Text* |
| NKJV | New King James Version |
| NRSV | New Revised Standard Version |
| OBT | Overtures to Biblical Theology |
| OTL | Old Testament Library |
| OTS | Old Testament Studies |
| *Presb* | *Presbyterion* |

| RSV | Revised Standard Version |
| SBLDS | Society of Biblical Literature Dissertation Series |
| SHBC | Smyth & Helwys Bible Commentary |
| *TDOT* | *Theological Dictionary of the Old Testament.* |
| *TLOT* | *Theological Lexicon of the Old Testament.* |
| TOTC | Tyndale Old Testament Commentaries |
| *TWOT* | *Theological Wordbook of the Old Testament* |
| UBCS | Understanding the Bible Commentary Series |
| WBC | Word Biblical Commentary |
| *WTJ* | *Westminster Theological Journal* |
| *ZAW* | *Zietschrift für die alttestamentliche Wissenschaft* |

# CONTRIBUTORS

**Phillip G. Camp, PhD**

(Union Theological Seminary and Presbyterian School of Christian Education). Associate Professor of Old Testament, Hazelip School of Theology at Lipscomb University.

**Andrew E. Hill, PhD**

(University of Michigan in Ann Arbor). Professor of Old Testament, Wheaton College.

**Brittany D. Kim, PhD**

(Wheaton College). Adjunct Professor, Ecclesia College; Adjunct Professor, Northeastern Seminary at Roberts Wesleyan College.

**Tremper Longman III, PhD**

(Yale University). Robert H. Gundry Professor of Biblical Studies, Westmont College.

**Claude Mariottini, PhD**

(Southern Baptist Theological Seminary). Professor of Old Testament, Northern Seminary.

## Elaine A. Phillips, PhD

(The Dropsie College for Hebrew and Cognate Learning). Professor of Biblical Studies, Gordon College.


## Wendy L. Widder, PhD

(University of the Free State). Research Associate, University of the Free State.


## John T. Willis, PhD

(Vanderbilt University). Professor of Old Testament, Abilene Christian University.


## Timothy M. Willis, PhD

(Harvard University). Professor of Religion, Pepperdine University.

# INTRODUCTION

Prayer plays a central role in the religious life and piety of ancient Israel, both on the individual and corporate levels. The Old Testament testifies to this fact by the pervasive presence of prayer, whether the presentation of actual prayers, descriptions of people praying, calls to pray, or critiques of prayer. In the Old Testament prayer takes a wide range of forms, including petition, praise, inquiry, intercession, cries for help, invoking of blessings, vow, lament, and confession, among others. Prayer touches on every facet of human life: religious, social, political, economic, personal.

Given the pervasiveness and complexity of prayer in biblical Israel, a close study of prayer in the Old Testament is vital to understanding Israel's and God's relationship, how Israel viewed God and themselves, and how prayer operates as a part of the worship life and daily life of Israelites. A study of prayer in the Old Testament also helps us understand what Israel thought happened in prayer—what God does in response to prayer and how the Israelites were shaped by their prayers.

## THE SCHOLARLY STUDY OF OLD TESTAMENT PRAYER

Given the pervasiveness of prayer in the Old Testament, the number of works focusing on prayer and the theology of prayer in the Old Testament is relatively small compared to other Old Testament topics and theological themes. Samuel Balentine noted this situation in his 1993 *Prayer in the Hebrew Bible:*

> On the one hand, to address the subject of prayer in scholarly publication, even when restricted to the relatively narrow confines of Hebrew Bible study, is to approach an area that historically has not been accorded much attention. It certainly has not occupied the passions and interests of Hebrew Bible scholars in the same way as other themes.[1]

Later in his book, Balentine observed, "From the middle of the nine-teenth century to the present, with few exceptions, prayer has not been a major subject in the development of Hebrew Bible theology."[2]

Almost twenty years later, Terence Fretheim made a similar observa-tion on the dearth of theological study and reflection on prayer in the Old Testament. In a footnote in his chapter "God, Faith, and the Practice of Prayer" in *Creation Untamed: The Bible, God, and Natural Disasters*, Fretheim says, "It is not common for prayer to be a topic in books on Old Testament theology. In my estimation, there is far too little sustained theological reflection on such a widespread Israelite practice."[3] Given that the third volume of John Goldingay's *Old Testament Theology* was pub-lished only the year before *Creation Untamed*, Fretheim may not have known that Goldingay dedicated an entire chapter, 132 pages, to prayer.[4] However, a survey of the tables of contents and indices of other major Old Testament theologies shows Goldingay to be the exception and con-firms Fretheim's general observation.[5]

Where prayer has played a role in Old Testament theology up to the publication of Balentine's book, scholars tended to focus on the psalms.[6] Claus Westermann's *Praise and Lament in the Psalms* is perhaps the most significant work on Old Testament prayer drawing on the psalms.[7] Moshe Greenberg's *Biblical Prose Prayer as a Window to the Popular Religion of Israel* and Ronald Clements's *In Spirit and in Truth: Insights from Bibli-cal Prayer* shift away from psalms to studies of the Old Testament prose prayers. Their studies, however, tend to be more sociological and psycho-logical than theological. Balentine's *Prayer in the Hebrew Bible* and Patrick Miller's *They Cried to the Lord: The Form and Theology of Biblical Prayer*, published the following year, represent a shift to a decidedly theological focus on the study of prayer that broadens beyond the psalms to the Old Testament as a whole. Miller's study still has a heavy focus on the psalms, but draws widely on the other parts of the Old Testament as well. Both works take a thematic approach, highlighting theological prayer themes and functions.

Some more recent works have focused on specific prayers in the Old Testament to discern important theological prayer themes. Among these are Ralph Hawkins's *While I Was Praying: Finding Insights about God in Old Testament Prayers*[8] and Walter Brueggemann's *Great Prayers of the Old Testament*.[9]

# THE PLACE OF THIS BOOK

The essays in this book are intended as a contribution to the study of the theology (or theologies) of prayer in the Old Testament by steering between the broad, sweeping overviews of prayer in the Old Testament as a whole and the more narrow focus on individual prayers. The contributions here focus on prayer in the major sections of the Old Testament, or, in some cases, individual books in order to discern their respective theologies of prayer. The sections selected are generally recognized divisions within Old Testament study, though in some cases, individual books fell outside the sections and are treated on their own. In each case, the focus is on the "final," canonical form of the text.[10]

By focusing on more narrow sections of the Old Testament, the goal is to discern the unique biblical voices on prayer within the larger Old Testament witness, while also recognizing the commonalities. The hope is that these essays will provide starting points and "grist for the mill" for further study of prayer in the Old Testament.

The articles, which are arranged largely according to the ordering of the Hebrew canon, are: The Pentateuch (Phillip G. Camp); The Deuteronomistic History (Timothy M. Willis); The Major Prophets—Isaiah, Jeremiah, and Ezekiel (John T. Willis); The Minor Prophets/Book of the Twelve (Andrew E. Hill); Psalms (Tremper Longman III); The Wisdom Literature—Job, Proverbs, and Ecclesiastes (Elaine A. Phillips); Ruth and Esther (Brittany D. Kim); Daniel (Wendy L. Widder); Chronicles, Ezra, and Nehemiah (Claude Mariottini).

This volume does not include studies of two books of the Old Testament. The first is Lamentations, though one can apply much of what Tremper Longman says about lament psalms to the series of laments in Lamentations. The second is Song of Songs (Song of Solomon). This omission may seem obvious given that the book does not mention God and has no obvious (or even obscure) prayer texts. In the pre-critical era, when allegorical and mystical interpretations were in vogue for Song of Songs, the union between the lover and the beloved could represent the longing of humanity to be joined to God and point to prayer as an avenue for that union.[11] Those who embrace the call to return to a pre-critical interpretation of the Song could make a similar case for finding a contribution to the theology of prayer in the Song.[12] Even scholars who reject allegorical readings of the Song may acknowledge that the discussion of human love and marriage in the Song, along with the biblical marriage metaphors of God and Israel or Christ and the Church, can lead us to reflect on the nature of our exclusive covenant relationship with God.[13] Despite the absence of prayer texts in the Song, such an openness to what it can teach us about a covenant relationship with God might also generate consideration of how prayer functions in maintaining and deepening that relationship.

## OLD TESTAMENT PRAYER AND THE CHRISTIAN LIFE

The practice of prayer, so vital to the religious life of ancient Israel, continues to play a primary role in the faith communities that claim the Jewish Scriptures as an abiding word of God to them today. As Clements observes:

> If the religion of ancient Israel was one that was characterized by a remarkable freedom and openness in its use of prayer, as the Old Testament testifies to us, then this has undoubtedly been one of its foremost legacies to the respective faiths of Judaism and Christianity. So many of the characteristic features of Jewish and Christian spirituality quite understandably have their roots in the way in which the Bible itself pictures men and women resorting to prayer.[14]

The authors in this book, as Christian interpreters of Scripture, believe that the Old Testament is the living word of God to the church. In that light, we recognize that the Old Testament teachings on prayer and what they reveal about the God to whom Israel prayed instruct the church and individual Christians as in prayer we go to God the Father, in the name of Jesus Christ his Son, through the Holy Spirit. Therefore, each author has addressed in some way how his or her discussion of the theology of prayer in a particular section of the Old Testament speaks to Christians today.

Our prayer as the editors of this book is not only that it will contribute to the ongoing scholarship on the theology of prayer in the Old Testament. We also pray that it will help believers today better understand and practice prayer in their own relationship with God, both individually and within their faith communities.

1. Samuel E. Balentine, *Prayer in the Hebrew Bible: The Drama of Divine-Human Dialogue*, in *OBT*, ed. Walter Brueggemann (Minneapolis: Fortress, 1993), 1.

2. Ibid., 226. Balentine surveys the theological treatment of prayer in the Old Testament to date on p. 226–259. He lists a few general critical studies of prayer, which he says "both confirm the general disinterest in this subject and seek to redress the situation with their own critical analyses" (p. 226; n. 1). Those studies are Moshe Greenberg, *Biblical Prose Prayer as a Window to the Popular Religion of Israel* (Berkeley: University of California Press, 1983); Ronald E. Clements, *In Spirit and in Truth: Insights from Biblical Prayer* (Atlanta: John Knox, 1985); Henning G. Reventlow, *Gebet im Alten Testament* (Stuttgart: Kohlhammer, 1986); Jack W. Corvin, "Stylistic and Functional Study of Prose Prayers in Historical Narratives of the Old Testament" (Ph.D. diss., Emory University, 1972); Edwin E. Staudt, "Prayer and the People in the Deuteronomist" (Ph.D. diss., Vanderbilt University, 1980).

3. Terence E. Fretheim, *Creation Untamed: The Bible, God, and Natural Disasters* (Grand Rapids: Baker, 2010), 124, n. 1. As resources on prayer, in the same note, he mentions Balentine's *Prayer in the Hebrew Bible* and Patrick D. Miller's *They Cried to the Lord: The Form and Theology of Biblical Prayer* (Minneapolis: Augsburg Fortress, 1994).

4. John Goldingay, *Old Testament Theology: Volume Three: Israel's Life* (Downers Grove: IVP Academic, 2009), 191–322. Chapter 3 is titled "Prayer and Thanksgiving."

5. Preuss has a small section on prayer in this OT theology. Horst D. Preuss, *Old Testament Theology*. Vol. II. (Louisville: Westminster John Knox, 1992). See 13.7 "Prayer," p. 245–250.

6. Balentine, *Prayer in the Hebrew Bible*, 235, 245–246.

7. Claus Westermann, *Praise and Lament in the Psalms*. (Atlanta: John Knox, 1981). Balentine says of this work, "Westermann has made the only effort to date to treat prayer as a major contributing element in the theology of the Hebrew Bible (*Prayer in the Hebrew Bible*, 243).

8. Ralph K. Hawkins, *While I Was Praying: Finding Insights about God in Old Testament Prayers* (Macon: Smyth & Helwys, 2006).

9. Walter Brueggemann, *Great Prayers of the Old Testament* (Louisville: Westminster John Knox, 2008).

10. In general, this means the text represented by the MT, though with appropriate text critical work when variant readings affect the meaning of the specific biblical texts addressed. We also recognized the difficulties associated with claims of final and canonical forms of biblical texts.

11. See the discussion of St. Francis de Sales's early 17th century interpretation of the Song of Solomon along these lines in Thomas F. Dailey, "A Song of Prayer: Reading the Canticle of Canticles with St. Francis de Sales," *Studia Mystica* 15:4 (1992): 65–82. In reference to de Sales's work in this regard, Dailey cites *Oeuvres de St. François de Sales*, Édition Complète 27 tomes (Annecy: J. Niéraut, 1893–19643), XXVI:10–19.

12. See, e.g., Robert W. Jenson, *Song of Songs*, in IBC, ed. James Luther Mays (Louisville: John Knox 2005), 1–15.

13. See, e.g., Tremper Longman III, *Song of Songs*, in *NICOT*, ed. Robert L. Hubbard Jr.(Grand Rapids: Eerdmans, 2001), 67–70.

14. Clements, *In Spirit and in Truth*, 3.

# PRAYER IN THE PENTATEUCH

## PHILLIP G. CAMP

## INTRODUCTORY ISSUES

The Pentateuch, or Torah, was central to shaping and maintaining ancient Israel's relationship to God, identity as the people of God, and mission in God's larger creative and redemptive purposes. While there is little direct instruction on prayer, the portrayal of prayer in the Pentateuch indicates that prayer was a vital component in living out the intent of the Torah in these matters.

Discerning what counts as prayer in the Pentateuch is not always easy. The specific vocabulary for prayer or intercession, from the Hebrew roots *pll* and *'tr*,[2] occurs a few times in the Pentateuch. Other terms suggesting prayer may be added: *tz'q*, "to cry out;"[3] *khlh*, "to appease;"[4] and in some cases *ydh*, "to confess."[5] But beyond specific vocabulary, there are a number of examples of prayer-like activity in the Pentateuch that use the usual vocabulary of speech (*'mr* or *qr'*).[6]

Defining prayer as conversation between humans and God[7] may work as a general and helpful concept of prayer, but it seems overly broad with respect to the Pentateuch. Does every conversation with God qualify as prayer? For the purposes of this study, I will use a definition of prayer that focuses on specific kinds of speech with or to God. So the working definition of prayer for this discussion will be "the act of petitioning, praising, giving thanks, or confessing to God."[8] This definition is broad enough to count some conversations as prayer, particularly those where specific petitions are made of God, but it is not so broad as to consider every conversation between God and humans as prayer.

# CONTEXTS FOR PRAYER TEXTS

In considering the theology of prayer in the Pentateuch, I want to contextualize the discussion in the larger presentation of God in the Pentateuch. For the sake of space, I will omit an in-depth discussion here and simply identify some of the major theological themes of the Pentateuch that will inform the discussion of prayer. Those themes are as follows: (1) God is creator and sovereign over creation; (2) God is one who blesses; (3) God is relational, including making promises and covenants; (4) God requires undivided loyalty on the part of his people; (5) God is just; (6) God is merciful.

Most instances of prayer in the Pentateuch occur within the narratives, though the covenant stipulations touch on prayer at times. Within the narratives the prayers serve, among other functions, as vehicles to convey the author's understanding of God.[9] The following are the primary contexts in which prayer texts occur.

## 1. Children/Family

Prayers in the Pentateuch frequently revolve around children and spouses. This focus for prayer makes sense in light of God's instruction for humans to "bear fruit, increase, and fill the earth"[10] (Gen 1:28; 9:1), and in light of God's promises to Israel's ancestors regarding numerous offspring and nations descending from them (e.g., Gen. 15:5; 17:6; 22:17; 26:4, 24; 28:14; 35:11). Thus, Abraham's prayers press God to fulfill the promises regarding offspring, in one way or another (15:1–21; 17:15–22). Abraham's servant prays that God will point out, through fulfillment of signs, the chosen wife for Isaac (24:12–14). Then Isaac intercedes ('tr) for his barren wife, Rebekah (25:21). In the naming of some of their children, Leah and Rachel acknowledge that God has heard, responded, and acted on their behalf in granting children to them (29:35; 30:6, 17–18, 22–23).

## 2. The Divine Promises/Covenant

Most of the prayers connected to the divine promises to the ancestors relate to children, but some prayers refer to the promises to the descendants of Abraham concerning possession the land and becoming a great nation (e.g., Gen. 12:2–3; 15:7; 17:8; 26:4; 28:13). So Abram will press God concerning those promises as well (15:8). Jacob's vow at Bethel is a response to Yahweh's reiteration of the covenant promises (Gen 28:10–22). Moses reminds God of the covenant promises as he pleads for Israel after they make the golden calf idol (Exod. 32:13; Deut. 9:27, 29). In the ritual prayer associated with giving the third-year tithe (Deut. 26:13–15), Israel calls on God to bless the people, invoking the promise to the ancestors with respect to the land.

## 3. Basic Necessities

Prayer language arises when people lack the basic necessities for survival. When Hagar and Ishmael run out of water in the desert, God responds to "the voice of the boy" (*qol hanna'ar*)[11] and points Hagar to water (Gen. 21:15–19). Moses also cries out (*tz'q*) to Yahweh concerning water for the community (Exod. 15:25; 17:4). In Moses' blessings on the Joseph tribes, he invokes the blessing of Yahweh that the land may be well watered and produce (Deut. 33:13–16).

## 4. Protection from a Human Threat/Enemy

Individuals and Israel as a whole pray when they find themselves under attack or vulnerable to potential attack. After God's curse makes Cain a fugitive and drives him from the land, Cain protests, "… anyone who finds me will kill me" (Gen. 4:13–16). As Jacob returns to Canaan, he is faced with the terrifying prospect of meeting his brother, Esau, from whom he had fled twenty years earlier because Esau wanted to kill him (Gen. 27:41–45). So Jacob asks God for deliverance from his brother (Gen. 32:9–12 [MT vv. 10–13]). A brief prayer, "For your salvation I wait, Yahweh," interrupts Jacob's blessings on his sons (Gen 49:18). Whether Jacob is praying for all Israel or only Dan is not clear, but, in either case, Jacob puts salvation in God's hands. As the Egyptian army traps Israel at the Red Sea, God interrupts Moses crying out (*tz'q*) to deliver them through the Red Sea (Exod. 14:10–18). This great deliverance then generates praise from Moses, Miriam, and the people (Exod. 15:1–21), and from Moses' father-in-law, Jethro (Exod. 18:10). Whenever the Ark of the Covenant moves ahead of the Israelite camp in the wilderness, Moses' regular practice is to invoke the protection of Yahweh at the start and end of the journey (Num. 10:35–36). In Moses' blessings on the tribes of Israel, he calls upon God to act against those who are hostile to the tribes of Judah and Levi (Deut. 33:7, 11).

## 5. Situations of Oppression/Abuse of Weak

A number of texts picture God as responding to the cries or needs of the oppressed and vulnerable. In Genesis 16:7–14, Hagar encounters "the angel of the LORD," a circumlocution for Yahweh, after she flees from Sarai, who "afflicted" her. Yahweh initiates their interaction by asking her where she has come from and where she is going. Hagar's response that she is fleeing from Sarai is not a petition per se, but the text indicates Yahweh understands an expression of distress behind her brief response in verse 11, which links her son's name, Ishmael, "Yahweh has heard (*shm'*)," to hearing her affliction. God likewise hears and responds to the cries and groans of Israel in their oppressive bondage in Egypt (Exod. 2:23–24; 5:22–6:8). Stipulations of the law in Exodus recognize that the oppressed widow or orphan will cry out (*tz'q*) to God (22:22–24 [MT vv. 21–23]), and likewise for the person whose cloak is taken in pledge but not returned by sundown (22:26–27 [MT vv. 25–26]). Similarly in Deuteronomy, one whose Hebrew "brother" will not lend to him in his need (15:9) and the worker who does not receive his daily wage (24:15) will "call out (*qr'*) against you to Yahweh."

## 6. Ritual/Cultic Contexts

A few texts dealing with cultic practices and worship rituals touch upon prayer. Three of these texts have the language of confession (*ydh*). Leviticus 5:5–6 connects confession of sins with sacrifice, and 16:21 links confession with putting the sins of the people on the scapegoat. The confessions could be understood not as an address to God but simply public declarations of sin to expose them. But they could also be viewed as ritual confessions, that is, prayers directed to God.[12] The priestly blessing in Numbers 6:24–25 invokes Yahweh's presence and care upon Israel. In the ceremony surrounding the discovery of a dead body, the elders of the nearest town pray (literally, "answer and say;" *we'anu we'ameru*) to declare their innocence in the matter and to effect atonement (Deut. 21:6–9). When Israelites offer the third-year tithe, they are commanded to say (*'mr*) to Yahweh that they have given the tithe as commanded and then they are to invoke Yahweh's blessings on Israel and their land (Deut. 26:13–15).

## 7. Divine Judgment

Stories of judgment provide the most frequent contexts for prayers in the Pentateuch. In some cases the judgment is against foreigners. In Genesis 18:22–33, Abraham pleads with God on behalf of any innocent ones who might be caught up in the judgment on Sodom and Gomorrah. As this judgment threatens to consume Lot and his family, Lot pleads with Yahweh[13] and is permitted to take refuge in Zoar (Gen. 19:15–22). When Abimelech, king of Gerar, takes Sarah as a wife (Gen. 20), God announces that he is a dead man. Abimelech protests his innocence, because he was tricked, and God acknowledges his innocence. So God instructs him to return Sarah to Abraham, who will then make intercession (*pll*) for Abimelech so that the women of his household can again bear children. On four occasions, Moses intercedes (*'tr*) on behalf of Pharaoh to relieve him of plagues God has inflicted on Egypt (Exod. 8:8–13 [MT vv. 4-9], 28–31 [MT vv. 24–27]; 9:27–33; 10:16–19).

Most of the time in the Pentateuch, however, the prayers in connection with judgment arise because of God's judgment upon Israelites. The story of Israel's worship of the golden calf image while at Mount Sinai provides the context for multiple prayers by Moses (Exod. 32–34; Deut. 9:9–10:11). Israel's repeated grumblings and rebellions in the wilderness evoke further judgment from Yahweh and repeated intercessions by Moses (Num. 11:1–3, 4–35). When Aaron and Miriam challenge Moses' authority, Yahweh strikes Miriam with a skin disease. At Aaron's urging, Moses then cries out (*tz'q*) for God to heal her (Num. 12:10–13). Then Israel's refusal to enter the land after the spies' report again leads to Yahweh's intention to destroy Israel and start over with Moses. Once more Moses pleads with Yahweh to relent and forgive the people (Num. 14:10–19). Finally, in the context of the curses of the covenant, God says that if the Israelites confess their sins and humble themselves, God will remember the covenant with the ancestors and remember the land (Lev. 26:40–42).

# THEOLOGICAL PRAYER THEMES IN THE PENTATEUCH

A study of the prayers discussed above reveals several theological themes with respect to prayer in the Pentateuch. Though not an exhaustive list, the following emerge as important themes.

## 1. God Is Available through Prayer

The prayer texts of the Pentateuch show a God who is present and ready to engage those who pray. Indeed, God often initiates the conversation (e.g., Gen. 16:7–8; 18:17–21; Exod. 32:7–10). In general, one does not require a priest, prophet, or other mediator to approach God. Individuals frequently engage God on their own. With respect to the servant's prayer in Genesis 24, Sarna says this text reveals the "concept of the individual as a religious unit" and one who can approach God on his/her own.[14] The servant's prayer, along with those of Hagar (Gen. 16:7–13) and Abimelech (Gen. 20:3–7), also demonstrates that prayer is not confined to the Abrahamic line. Furthermore, men and women pray, showing that this access to God is not gender specific.

However, within the Pentateuch, prayers for forgiveness and to avert God's judgment involve a mediator, either a prophetic figure like Abraham (Gen. 18:22–33; 20:7, 17) or Moses (Exod. 8:8–13 [MT vv. 4–9], 28–31 [MT vv. 24–27]; 9:27–33; 10:16–19; Exod. 32–34; Num. 14:10–25), or a priest in connection with confession of sin and sacrifice (Lev. 5:5–6; 16:21). While it may be too strong to say that prayers for forgiveness *require* an intercessor, the Pentateuch at least indicates that mediators appointed by God successfully advocate for those under judgment and that God, in his mercy, places an intermediary between himself and the people as a buffer for his judgment.[15]

## 2. Prayer Expresses a Dependence on God for Survival and Well-Being

The prayers of the Pentateuch reveal the dependence of weak, relatively powerless people (or those made powerless), whose survival remains a constant question apart from the power and favor of Yahweh. For example, Cain (Gen. 4:10–14) and Jacob (32:9–12 [MT 10–13]) pray because they fear someone will kill them, and they are powerless to save themselves. When the Ark of the Covenant is moved as Israel sets out, Moses says, "Arise, Yahweh, let your enemies be scattered, and those who hate you flee before you." Then, when it comes to rest as Israel encamps, Moses calls for Yahweh to return. These are prayers for God's protecting presence with the vulnerable camp on the move (Num. 10:35–36). The Israelites and Moses cry out for drinkable water (Exod. 15:25) or simply water to drink (Exod. 17:1–7; Num. 20:1–13) because they have no means to procure this necessity in the wilderness. The priestly blessing (Num. 6:24–26) recognizes Israel's ongoing need for Yahweh's blessing, protection, presence, graciousness, and peace. These prayers reveal the expectation that God can or will do for them what they cannot do for themselves.[16]

### 3. God Invites and Accepts Intercession on Behalf of Others

God's willingness to accept intercession is evident throughout the Pentateuch. The intercession could be for individuals within the covenant people, such as Isaac's intercession for his barren wife (Gen. 25:21). Intercession could also be for foreigners, for example, the innocent ones who might have been in Sodom and Gomorrah (Gen 18:22–33), Abimelech (Gen. 20:17–18), and Pharaoh (Exod. 8:8–13 [MT vv. 4–9], 28–31 [MT vv. 24–27]; 9:27–33; 10:16–19). Intercession can be for Israel as a whole, as illustrated by two major examples: the golden calf story in Exodus 32–34 (cf. Deut. 9:20–10:11) and God's response to Israel's refusal to take the land in light of the spies' report in Numbers 14.

A plausible reading of God's demand that Moses "leave him alone," so that he can destroy the people (Exod. 32:10), is as an invitation for Moses to intercede. In Balentine's words, it is "an invitation by prohibition,"[17] or, with Childs, God "leaves the door open for intercession."[18] One can read God's threat to destroy Israel and start over with Moses in Numbers 14:12 in a similar way.[19] In such cases, God could have executed judgment without saying anything to the intercessors, so God speaking to them beforehand implies their intercession "can and will affect things."[20]

### 4. Prayer Can Question and Challenge God

Prayer in the Pentateuch often moves beyond petition to direct, though usually deferential, challenges to God, beginning with Cain's protest,

"My punishment is greater than I can bear" (Gen. 4:13). Abram challenges God's assurance of great reward with the protest, "You have not given me offspring" (Gen. 15:3). Lot refuses the command to head for the hills ("Oh, no, my lords") and protests, though with deference, that he cannot accomplish what he has been told to do (Gen. 19:18). So also Moses pointedly challenges God in prayer in his attempts to avoid his call in Exodus 3–4. Whether the whole of the dialogue can be considered prayer, Moses' refusal has a petition quality: "Please send someone else" (4:13). In this case, God reacts to the prayer emotionally, not with compassion but with anger, though God does condescend to the protest by sending Aaron.

In both cases where God resolves to destroy Israel and start over with Moses (Exod. 32–33; Num. 14), Moses pushes back against God. In Exodus 32:7-14 (cf. Deut. 9:26), Moses refuses responsibility for the people and puts it back on God: "*Your* people, whom *you* brought out." (Exod. 32:12; cf. v. 7). Moses emphasizes his protest by twice referring to what God intends to do as "evil" (*ra'ah*).[21] In both stories, Moses appeals to the divine reputation, essentially saying, "What will people say about you if you do this—that you can start but not complete your plan?"

Even more striking is Moses accusation against God in Exodus 5:22–23, where he speaks to (or against[22]) God and, to an extent, equates God with Pharaoh. Moses accuses God of causing "evil" (*ra'a'*) upon his people just as Pharaoh brought "evil" (*ra'a'*) upon the people. Moses also protests to God over the personal burden or danger in dealing with Israel (Exod. 17:4; 33:12; Num. 11:11).

Prayer sometimes pushes even further, questioning whether God is really just. For example, in Genesis 18:22–33, Abraham protests God's planned destruction of Sodom and Gomorrah. Abraham is deferential,[23] but the sharpness of the protest is indicated by his double use of "indeed" (*'af*, vv. 23–24) and by the use of, "far be that from you" (*khalilah*; v. 25). Then his challenge gets even more direct as he asks, "Will the judge of all the earth not do justice?" (v. 25). The implication is clear: if Yahweh destroys the righteous with the wicked, he is not just. The story of Abimelech taking Sarah as a wife echoes the Sodom and Gomorrah story as the king protests by asking whether God will destroy an innocent nation (Gen. 20:3–7). A similar question of God's justice arises during Korah's rebellion when Moses asks God whether one person's sin will lead God to be angry with and consume the whole congregation (Num 16:20–22).

Such instances of passionate engagement between the petitioner and God reveal a real, living relationship between them. God's servants are not machines who simply carry out instructions. Rather they are those who interact with, protest, and suggest. While the ones praying normally show deference to God, they are also bold, tenacious, and hold God to his own promises and standard of justice. They insist that God act in ways that are consistent with his character in general, as they understand it.[24] God accepts such protests and challenges and responds, though not always as the servant might wish (see below).

## 5. God Answers Prayers but as God Sees Fit: God Remains Sovereign

Often God responds to prayer and graciously gives what is asked. Even more, prayer can persuade or move God to alter his original intentions and purposes. As Balentine observes with respect to Numbers 14: "Put simply, Moses' prayer influences the outcome of the story."[25] In Exodus 32:12, Moses asks God to relent or change his mind (*nkhm*) concerning the evil (*r'h*) he intends to bring upon the people. The prayer has the desired effect as God alters his announced plan: "Yahweh relented (*nkhm*) concerning the evil (*r'h*) that he said he would do to his people" (Exod. 32:14). Such responses indicate that God takes seriously the challenges and arguments of those who engage him. As Fretheim notes in light of Moses' prayer in Exodus 32, "God treats the relationship with the people with an integrity that is responsive to what they do and say."[26]

Within the cultic context, God responds to prayers of confession, leading to forgiveness (Lev. 5:5–6; 16:21; Num. 5:6–7), and to declarations of innocence before God, resulting in atonement (Deut. 21:7–8). One should not, however, consider such prayers magical, as though they force God's hand. The decision to forgive always rests with God. Moses seems to recognize this in Exodus 32:30 when he says, "*perhaps* (*'ulay*) I can make atonement for your [Israel's] sin."[27]

Indeed, prayer in no way manipulates or forces God to act. Though prayer is relational, it is not a relationship of equals. God is Creator and the initiator of covenant relationship, who remains the sovereign party in the relationship. Prayer engages God, reasons and argues with God, and lays the petitions and requests before God. But God is free to answer a prayer in part or in whole, to delay answering, to give an unexpected answer, or to say "no."[28]

Several texts in the Pentateuch reveal this understanding of prayer. Jacob's brief prayer in the midst of his blessings on his sons, "For your salvation I wait, Yahweh" (Gen. 49:18), demonstrates that prayer does not put God on one's own timetable, but the reverse. When Abraham asks essentially that Ishmael be counted as the promised child, the answer is "no." It will be Sarai's child, though God will bless Ishmael (Gen. 17:17–21). Moses begs God to send someone other than him to bring the Israelites out of Egypt, but God insists on Moses going, though with the partial concession that Aaron will now serve as Moses' spokesman (Exod. 4:13–17). In Exodus 32:30–34, Moses returns to God to ask for forgiveness for all Israel in light of their idolatry. Again God's response is "no," those who have sinned will be blotted out of God's book. As Childs says, "God let himself be persuaded, but here there is no room for negotiation. God rejects Moses' plea for a full forgiveness."[29] In Exodus 33:12–23, God partially fulfills Moses' requests. God agrees to go with Israel as Moses asks, but rather than seeing God's glory he can see God's goodness, not God's face but God's back. God explains his refusal as a means to protect Moses from death, which would result if he saw God's face.[30] When Moses entreats God to let him enter the land, God pointedly rejects the petition: "Enough! Do not continue to speak to me of this matter!" (Deut. 3:23–26). Even Moses, the great intercessor for Israel, does not get all that he asks for every time.

## 6. God Is Attuned to the Prayers of the Vulnerable and Oppressed

God's response to the prayers of the vulnerable and oppressed fits naturally with the thematic dominance of the Exodus in the Pentateuch, where God hears and responds to the cries and groaning of Israel under oppression in Egypt (Exod. 2:23–24 with 3:7–10; Exod. 6:5; Num. 20:16). In this light, note also the prayer of Hagar (Gen. 16:7–14), whose plight in many ways parallels and anticipates Israel's plight in Egypt.[31] As noted in the discussion of contexts above, a few of the laws in the Pentateuch also reveal God's attention to the prayers of the poor and oppressed, specifically, the widow and orphan (Exod. 22:22–23 [MT vv. 21–23]), the neighbor whose garment is taken in pledge and not returned by sundown (22:26–27 [MT vv. 25–26]), the Israelite "brother" who is refused a loan (Deut. 15:9), and a poor worker who is not paid (Deut. 24:15). In both of the laws from Exodus, Israel is told that God will "hear" the cries of those so oppressed, and in both laws from Deuteronomy, the result is that it will be counted as sin/guilt (*kht*) against the offender.

Thus, prayer creates an ethical impulse that should shape Israel's response to the oppressed. However, if Israelites oppress as they were oppressed by the Egyptians, then, as in the Exodus story, the oppressed will cry out to God. When they do, God will count the Israelite oppressors guilty as he did the Egyptians, with the implication that judgment will follow.

## 7. Prayer Expands One's Vision beyond the Immediate, Obvious, and Possible to What God Can Do

Prayer in the Pentateuch opens one's eyes to the power of God and the future God is creating. In fact, the Pentateuch, by opening with God's creative activity—his shaping of, sovereignty over, and ongoing participation within creation—provides the larger context to opening this prayerful imagination.

Abram protests his childlessness and asks God how he will know that he shall possess the land. In response, God does not explain *how* he will do things. Instead, God invites Abraham to contemplate the stars in the heavens: "Now look heavenward. Count the stars if you are able to count them. Thus will be your offspring" (Gen. 15:5). God also points Abram's vision, not to the next year or a few years down the road, but to his intentions 400 years in the future (Gen. 15:13–21). As Brueggemann notes, God expands Abram's vision beyond the immediate circumstances and what he imagines is possible by having him contemplate the "activity of the creator which transports the man's gaze from the narrow horizon of human events."[32] The same idea is present in Genesis 17:15–22, where Abraham laughs at God's claim that Sarai will have a baby because they are both far too old. God rejects Abraham's practical, present alternative in Ishmael and insists that a son through Sarai will fulfill the covenant. Abraham is again pushed to look beyond his own understanding to the possibilities and power of God. This episode then anticipates God's response to Sarah's laughter, "Is anything too wonderful (or difficult) for Yahweh?" (Gen. 18:14).

After Moses' attempt to liberate his fellow Israelites seems at a dead end, he complains to God (Exod. 5:22–23). God responds, "Now you will see what I will do to Pharaoh," and God opens (or reopens) a vista for Moses that goes beyond the present circumstances not only to the overcoming of Egypt and the Exodus, but to the possession of the land (Exod. 6:1–8). Then in Exodus 14:15–18, when Israel is backed against the Red Sea with the Egyptian army pressing, God tells Moses to stop crying out (stop praying?), turn around, and watch God do the impossible: make a path through the sea. Later, when Moses cries out to God over lack of water—really, over the possibility of being stoned for lack of water—God sends him to the most unlikely place for water: a rock (Exod. 17:1–7). Finally, note the interaction between God and Moses in the wilderness in Numbers 11:21–23 when Moses protests the impossibility of God's promise to provide overabundant meat for the great multitude of Israelites. Moses' mind can only conceive conventional means of providing meat. But God responds, "Is the LORD'S power limited?[33] Now you shall see whether my word will come true for you or not" (NRSV). Moses' power is limited in such matters, but not God's. The call in such prayers is not to solve or fix the problem oneself but to imagine and trust in what the all-powerful God of Israel can do.

## 8. Prayer Bears Witness to the God of Israel

In the Pentateuch, prayer is sometimes connected to the witness or reputation of Yahweh. For example, Jethro's burst of praise upon hearing Moses' reports of what God had done to the Egyptians bears witness to the power of Israel's God: "Blessed be Yahweh, who has delivered you from the hands of the Egyptians and the hand of Pharaoh" (Exod. 18:10). In this case, God's power leads to a foreigner, a Midianite, bearing witness. In a similar fashion, the Song of Moses—if it can be considered a prayer of praise—declares in its praise that what God had done to Egypt would make Yahweh's reputation known among the peoples Israel would encounter, generating fear and dread among them (Exod. 15:12–16).

In some cases, witness is part of the appeal to Yahweh to respond to a petition, for example, in Moses' intercessions for Israel in Exodus 32–33 and Numbers 14. Moses raises the possibility in Exodus 32:12 that the

Egyptians will say that God brought out Israel to kill them. In Numbers 14:15–16, Moses asserts that if God destroys Israel, the nations will conclude that God could take Israel out of Egypt but could not bring them into the land. Moses' argument suggests that if God goes through with his intentions, it will be a negative witness about God to others.

Whether such appeals trigger God's response is unclear—Moses could be saying anything and everything to try to convince God to relent—but the prayer still raises the question of witness. That these appeals do move God is suggested by the fact that, in other cases, God answers petitions precisely to make his name or reputation known. Note, for example, that when Moses agrees to petition Yahweh on Pharaoh's behalf to rid the land of the frogs, Moses says it is so Pharaoh will "know that there is no one like Yahweh our God" (Exod. 8:10 [MT v. 6]). Similarly, when Moses petitions for the thunder and hail to stop, it is so Pharaoh "will know that the earth belongs to Yahweh" (Exod. 9:29). Even Pharaoh's requests for Moses to intercede with Yahweh imply an acknowledgement that this God can do something neither Pharaoh nor the gods of Egypt can do. Pharaoh must give "at least a tacit acknowledgement of the Yahweh he has earlier claimed not to know."[34]

Deuteronomy 4:7 presents a clear connection between prayer and witness. It is precisely answered prayer, along with the wisdom and righteousness revealed in the Torah, that will separate Yahweh from the gods of the nations: "For what great nation has gods so near to it as Yahweh our God is [to us] whenever we call to him?" The wording suggests that it is not just a witness to the nations, however, but also a witness or reassurance to Israel that their God is superior to those of the nations.

## PRAYERS IN THE PENTATEUCH AND OUR PRAYERS TODAY

In our own prayers we encounter this same God of the Pentateuch, the sovereign creator who blesses, enters covenant relationship, and calls his people to be a blessing. This same God has called us into a new covenant relationship with him through Jesus Christ, who is the fulfillment of the OT Law (Matt. 5:17–18). He continues to make himself available to us and others through prayer, regardless of social position, nationality, gender, or other such factors. We approach God in prayer because we, like Israel, depend on God for our survival and well-being. We pray not only for ourselves, but we also petition God on behalf of others. In those intercessions for others, we are pointed to Jesus, the great high priest, and to the Spirit who intercedes for us before the Father (Rom. 8:26–27; Heb. 7:25). The Pentateuch also shows us that this God is attuned to and responds to the cries of the vulnerable, and we are called to be as well.

The Pentateuch reminds us of what we see elsewhere in the Bible but may be timid about in our own practice: in prayer we are permitted to engage and challenge God over what seems impossible or unjust to us. We do so with respect, remembering that prayer is not a conversation of equals. But that is precisely why we take the complaints to God. We believe he should and can do something about it. We do so boldly because we are truly in a relationship with God, who takes our concerns seriously and responds to them.

In this light, we see that God not only answers prayers, but is also free to answer when and how he sees fits. So we are called to trust in his sovereignty in these matters. Indeed, though his response may not be the answer that we want (or think we want), through prayer God can open our eyes to "so much more than we can ask or imagine" (Eph. 3:20). Our prayers to God in our dependence and our praise to God in light of his responses continue then to serve as a witness within the community of faith and to the world of the amazing God we serve.

---

1. The root *pll* occurs in Gen. 20:7, 17; Num. 11:2; 21:7 (2x); Deut. 9:20, 26.

2. The root *'tr* occurs in Gen. 25:21 (2x); Exod. 8:8, 9, 28, 29, 30 [MT 8:4, 5, 24, 25, 26]; 9:28; 10:17, 18.

3. For the root *tz'q* in prayer contexts, see Exod. 8:8; 14:10, 15; 15:25; 17:4; 22:23, 27 [MT 22:22, 26]; Num. 11:2; 12:13; 20:16. Exod. 2:23 uses the related root *z'q*. On *tz'q* as prayer language ("the most emotionally colored of all expressions for 'to pray'"), see *TLOT* 3:1092.

4. In reference to prayer, the piel of *khlh* occurs in the Pentateuch only in Exod. 32:11. For similar uses, see, e.g, 1 Sam. 13:12; 1 Kings 13:6; Dan. 9:13; Zech. 7:2; 8:21.

5. For *ydh*, see Gen. 29:35; Lev. 5:5; 16:21; 26:40; Num. 5:7.

6. For *'mr* see, e.g., Gen. 4:13; 15:2; 16:8; 19:18; Exod. 5:22; Num. 10:35; 11:11; Deut 26:13. For *qr'* see, e.g., Deut. 15:9; 24:15.

7. See, e.g., Samuel E. Balentine, *Prayer in the Hebrew Bible: The Drama of Divine-Human Dialogue*, OBT (Minneapolis: Fortress, 1993), 30.

8. Arland J. Hultgren, "Prayer," in *HCBD*, ed. Mark Alan Powell 875.

9. Along these lines, see Balentine, *Prayer in the Hebrew Bible*, 89–90.

10. Unless otherwise noted, the translations of OT texts are mine.

11. Verse 16 says that Hagar "lifted her voice and wept." However, the text twice says that God "heard" the boy's voice (twice noted in v. 17). In v. 16, the LXX says that "they," Hagar and Ishmael, lifted their voices and wept. That the text makes explicit the response to the boy's voice does not rule out that God responded also to Hagar's weeping.

12. Jacob Milgrom suggests the first instance (5:5–6) could be directed to God, since God is the offended party (*Leviticus*, AB 3 (New York: Doubleday, 1991), 303. On confession of sin as bringing the sin to light, see Baruch A. Levine, *Leviticus* in JPSTC, ed. Nahum M. Sarna (Skokie, IL: Jewish Publication Society, 1989), 23.

13. The conversation could be between Lot and the angels or Lot and Yahweh. But the use of "I" in verses 21–22 points to Yahweh since verses 13 and 24–25 indicate it is Yahweh who overthrows the cities, and so Yahweh is the one who could spare a city among them.

14. Nahum M. Sarna, *Genesis*, JPSTC (Skokie: Jewish Publication Society, 1989), 158–59.

15. L. Paul Moore, "Prayer in the Pentateuch," *BSac* 98:391 (1941): 332.

16. Goldingay discusses the relationship between God and Israel (or the Israelite petitioner) in terms of an ideal master-servant relationship, which is more "covenantal or familial" than "contractual." The servant depends on the master for care and the master is expected to provide it. So the servant can appeal to the master for relief. In this respect, he notes Gen 24; Exod 5:15, 22-23; Num11:11. John Goldingay, *Old Testament Theology: Volume Three: Israel's Life* (Downers Grove: IVP Academic, 2009), 203-205.

17. Balentine, *Prayer in the Hebrew Bible*, 136.

18. Brevard Childs, *The Book of Exodus*, OTL, eds. Peter Ackroyd, James Barr, John Bright, G. Ernest Wright (Louisville: Westminster, 1974), 567.

19. Jacob Milgrom, *Numbers*, JPSTC (Skokie: Jewish Publication Society, 1989), 83; Balentine, *Prayer in the Hebrew Bible*, 134.

20. Patrick D. Miller, "Prayer and Divine Action," in *God in the Fray: A Tribute to Walter Brueggemann*, ed. Tod Linafelt and Timothy K. Beal (Minneapolis: Fortress, 1988), 218-19. Miller is discussing Exodus 32.

21. Balentine notes a third reference to "evil" (r'h) narrator in 31:14 (*Prayer in the Hebrew Bible*, 137).

22. Durham translates 5:22, "So Moses turned on Yahweh," noting that the preposition 'el could mean "toward" but also has the senses of "against" and "upon" (John I. Durham, *Exodus*, in WBC 3, ed. John D.W. Watts (Waco: Word Books, 1987), 67, 69.

23. He twice addresses God as "lord" ('adonay; vv. 30, 31), three times uses "please" (na', vv. 27, 30, 31) and refers to himself as "dust and ashes" (v. 27).

24. See, e.g., Christopher Wright, *Deuteronomy*, in NIBC 4, ed. F.F. Bruce (Peabody: Hendrickson, 1996), 139; Patrick D. Miller, *Deuteronomy*, IBC (Louisville: John Knox, 1990), 123–24.

25. Ballentine, *Prayer in the Hebrew Bible*, 132.

26. Terence E. Fretheim, *Exodus*, IBC (Louisville: John Knox, 1991), 287. He goes on to say that God's openness to prayer and the future demonstrate what in God's character is "unchangeable": his steadfast love, his faithfulness to promises, and his will for everyone's salvation. Cf. Childs, *Exodus*, 568.

27. Cf. similar uses of 'ulay in Amos 5:15 and in Zeph. 2:3.

28. Goldingay (*Old Testament Theology Vol. 3*, 233) says that, in the OT, God's "no" is not absolute and normally involves "both yes and no." E.g., no, Moses cannot go into the land, but, yes, he can see it; no, Ishmael will not fulfill God's covenant promises to Abraham, but, yes, God will bless him.

29. Childs, *Exodus*, 572.

30. Durham, *Exodus*, 452.

31. For parallels between Hagar's and Israel's stories, see Tikva Frymer-Kensky, *Reading the Women of the Bible: A New Interpretation of Their Stories* (New York: Schocken Books, 2002), 233.

32. Walter Brueggemann, *Genesis*, IBC (Atlanta: John Knox, 1982), 143.

33. Literally, "Is the hand of Yahweh short?"

34. Durham, *Exodus*, 104. See Exod 5:2.

# PRAYER IN THE DEUTERONOMISTIC HISTORY

## TIMOTHY WILLIS

Modern Old Testament scholars apply the label "Deuteronomistic History" (DtrH) to the books of Joshua through 2 Kings (excluding Ruth). These six books relate the central history of Israel as a nation, from the days of its entry into the Promised Land under the leadership of Joshua until its exile from the land at the hands of Babylonian invaders. This is the social and political situation that the book of Deuteronomy envisions, and the DtrH often uses language and themes from Deuteronomy to relate the successes and failures of Israel's leaders, as they strive to lead the people in living out the vision that Moses lays before them in Deuteronomy. The narrative focuses the reader's attention primarily on Israel's national leaders—Joshua, the judges, and then the kings—all the while highlighting ways in which prophets repeatedly call them to genuine obedience to the Law of Moses, the nation's first leader. The focus on leaders is not designed to excuse the people from covenantal responsibilities; instead, they are examples of faith or failure, whose fates stand as an encouragement or warning to all.

## VERBAL RELATIONSHIP WITH GOD

There are a handful of expressions found in the DtrH that indicate the human voices in a dialogue with God, what we might broadly call "prayer."[1] Most are petitions for divine help or knowledge. Several individuals "call [*qara*] on (the name of) the LORD" in times of need

(Judg. 15:18; 16:28; 1 Sam. 12:17; 1 Kings 17:20; 18:24; 2 Kings 5:11; 20:11), others "seek the favor of [*hillah pene*] the LORD" (1 Sam. 13:12; 1 Kings 13:6; 2 Kings 13:4).[2] Solomon repeatedly entreats the Lord to "hear . . . the prayer and plea" (*shema'... tepillah we-tehinnah*) of those who turn and worship him at the Temple (1 Kings 8:28, 30, 33, 38, 45, 49). Individuals and groups "ask" (*sha'al*—e.g., Josh. 9:14; Judg. 1:1; 20:23, 27; 1 Sam. 1:20, 27; 2:20; 10:22; 22:10; 23:2, 4; 28:6; 30:8; 2 Sam. 2:1; 5:19, 23) or "inquire" (*darash*—e.g., 1 Sam. 9:9; 1 Kings 22:5, 8; 2 Kings 3:11; 8:8; 22:13, 18) of the Lord when they need help or reassurance or information.[3] One minor issue of form concerns whether petitioners speak with the Lord directly or employ an intermediary (prophet, priest) to speak for them (see 1 Sam. 23:9–11). On at least two occasions the people specifically ask Samuel to "pray for us" ("on our behalf"—1 Sam. 7:5; 12:19, 23), but Hannah obviously voices her own prayers (1 Sam. 1:12–13). It appears that either mode is acceptable.

The discussion that follows limits the scope of investigation to those passages that employ the Hebrew root *pll*, either in its verb form ("pray" = *hitpallel*) or its noun form ("prayer" = *tepillah*). Four passages report prayers of sufficient length to allow for detailed consideration of themes within them.[4] Three of the four prayers come from the lips of righteous kings—David (2 Sam. 7:18–29), Solomon (1 Kings 8:14–53), and Hezekiah (2 Kings 19:15–19). These three fit well the category of "formal prayers" as described by Balentine.[5] All three illustrate the principle that leaders in the DtrH can serve as positive role models for the people. Hannah the mother of Samuel speaks the fourth prayer (1 Sam. 2:1–10), and she highlights some of the same themes that stand out in the three royal prayers, a fact that also illustrates how the prayers of the nation's leaders might serve as models for the prayers of all pious Israelites.[6] For the sake of brevity, I will devote more comments to the Prayer of David in 2 Samuel 7:18–29, and then I will briefly show how some of the characteristics I distill from David's prayer also appear in the prayers of the other two kings and Hannah (1 Kings 8:14–66; 2 Kings 19:14–19; 1 Sam. 2:1–10).

## THE HISTORICAL SETTING

The Prayer of David stands as the final scene in a series of events that take place in Jerusalem, as David captures the city and makes it his capital and the center of worship in Israel (2 Sam. 5:6–7:29). Two overlapping themes from the book of Exodus provide important pieces to the backdrop of the report about these events: God performs awesome wonders in the Exodus to deliver his people from slavery, and what motivates him to deliver his people from slavery is his deep desire to dwell among his people (Exod. 15:1–18; 25:8; 29:45–46). We see the culmination of God's plans to dwell among his people when David brings the Ark of the Covenant to Jerusalem (2 Samuel 6). The desire for a "permanent residence" for the Ark of the Covenant points to greater certitude regarding the presence of God among his people. Under David's leadership—and for the first time in Israel's history—the entire land that the Lord had promised to Abraham has come under Israel's control. David has made Jerusalem his capital and built a royal palace there, and now he acts to place the Ark of God under his direct care. Following a small bump in the road, both literally and figuratively, he brings the Ark of God into the City of David and places it inside its own special tent, making God and his ark the centerpiece of David's kingdom.

But David is not satisfied. He voices his discomfort to the prophet Nathan at the beginning of 2 Samuel 7 saying, "See now, I dwell in a house of cedar, but the ark of God dwells in a tent." The dwelling place of the Lord should be more "established." The Lord has secured the land for Israel, and the Lord's permanent residence among the Israelites should reflect this fact. But then the Lord speaks to Nathan in a dream and asks why David is concerned about the kind of structure in which God "dwells" (v. 5). He tells Nathan that David will not build a house for the Lord; instead, the Lord promises to "establish" David's house first (vv. 12–13), and then the Lord will have David's son build a house for the Lord.

The Lord's answer and promise drive David to his knees in prayer. Just when David is moving to put the Lord "front and center" in his kingdom, the Lord acts to put David and David's house "front and center." The interplay between the kingship of David (and his descendants) and the kingship of Yahweh stands as a central issue throughout the remainder of the DtrH, and it seems that the compiler of the DtrH uses this and other formal prayers to convey the proper attitude for Israel's kings to have about this interplay. As Balentine observes, the covenant relationship between the Lord and his people involves a dialogue, "a genuine partnership" based on reciprocity and a mutual responsibility to maintain the relationship.[7] The Lord promises to be their God, and Israel promises to be his people. Both must act faithfully to sustain the covenant.

# THE PRAYER OF DAVID

At least four themes in the Prayer of David deserve extended comment. The most pervasive theme is that *the earthly king assumes the attitude of a servant.* Two complementary rhetorical features in the prayer project this attitude. The first feature is David's self-designation as "your servant," a term that he employs no less than ten times in this prayer of twelve verses. Referring to oneself as "your servant" is well known in the Bible as a respectful mode of address to one of superior status, particularly in the presence of a king (1 Sam. 17:32, 34, 36; 22:15; 28:21; 2 Sam. 9:2, 6, 11; 11:21, 24; 13:24, 35; 14:6, 7, 12, 15, 17, 19, 20, 22; 15:2, 8, 21, 34; 18:29; 19:19, 20, 26–28, 35–37). It is obviously significant that King David, praying in the presence of the Divine King, abandons the typical royal posturing and assumes the role of the servant. He does not recall past exploits on the battlefield or accomplishments as an administrator or even acts of sincere piety; instead, he highlights the wondrous mercy and blessings showered on him by the Lord. David is who he is because of the beneficence of his King.

The second rhetorical feature to convey the attitude of the Davidic king as royal servant is less obvious. David addresses God eight times in this prayer with the double name, "Lord GOD"[8] (*'adonay yhwh*). There are only five other examples of this double name in the rest of the DtrH (Josh. 7:7; Judg. 6:22; 16:28; 1 Kings 2:26; 8:53). The name presents an interesting dilemma for translators. The common English translation ("Lord GOD") reflects the Qere form of the Masoretic Text (what is audibly read), but this does not match the Kethibh form (what is visually written). During the Second Temple Period, Jewish leaders adopted various oral substitutes to avoid voicing the divine name, and the most prevalent alternative is *'adonay* ("the Lord"). The dilemma comes when the proper name is paired in the original text with the term that later comes to stand in its place. Once it became accepted to render the consonantal text of *yhwh* with the vocalized reading of *'adonay*, the double name in the Hebrew consonantal text looks redundant. One naturally would read the Kethibh form as "Adonay Adonay." Some Greek translations of the

Hebrew Bible do exactly that in other passages, reading this as a duplicative proper name, *kurie kurie*. Others render the two terms with a single *kurie*, while some transliterate the first term from Hebrew to Greek and read *adonai kurie*. At least, that is what they do in every other passage in the OT. But for some reason the Greek translators do not do that in David's prayer. Here, and only here in the entire LXX, instead of reading *kurie kurie* or *kurie* or *adonai kurie*, the Greek translators render the double name as *kurie mou kurie* ("my lord the Lord"). To put it another way, in David's prayer virtually all Greek translations reflect a Hebrew forerunner that reads *'adoni Yahweh*, rather than following the traditional rendering of *'adonay Yahweh*.[9]

It is in this Greek rendering that we recognize the second way in which David addresses God as king. Many individuals in the OT address a king as "my lord the king" or "my lord David/Ahab/etc." If we adopt the Greek translation in this passage (which probably reflects the earliest transmission tradition), we see that David is imitating the standard conventions for addressing an important figure, particularly a king. The reason why someone would read it this way is obvious: "my lord Yahweh" functions as a complement to David's frequent reference to himself as "your servant." These two terms show how David adopts court language to convey his genuine humility. The king of Israel is assuming the proper posture before his superior, the Divine King.

The second theme of David's prayer becomes clear when we consider the general flow of thought in the prayer. The theme is that *a petitioner's confident appeal regarding the future rests in his/her knowledge of the Lord's deeds in the past*. David's prayer falls into two halves: verses 18–24 and verses 25–29. The first half consists of praise; the second half shifts to petition. The train of thought in the first half is conducted forward by three rhetorical questions (vv. 18, 20, 23), while the second half progresses through a threefold series of requests that begin with "and now" (*we-'attah*; vv. 25, 28, 29). This demarcation matches the general flow of thought in the prayer. David praises the Lord in the first half of the prayer for his dealings in the past, and in the second half he expresses his confidence regarding how he would like the Lord to deal with him (and his house) in the future.

The first half of the prayer indelibly ties the Lord's past dealings with David to the Lord's past dealings with the entire nation. The first two rhetorical questions (vv. 18 and 20) express David's amazement at the Lord's dealings with him. "Who am I ... and what is my house ...?" "What more can David say to you?" The third rhetorical question (v. 23) expresses amazement at the Lord's prior dealings with the nation. "And who is like your people Israel ...?" The amazing acts that the Lord has performed recently for David are comparable to the amazing acts he had performed previously for all Israel. This implies that the covenant the Lord is establishing with David is at least based on the same principles as the covenant he inaugurated with Israel at Sinai, and it is possible that David/ the writer wishes to incorporate the dynastic promise to David into that earlier covenant. As a prime example of this notion, David closes the first half of the prayer in verse 24 by mentioning that the Lord "established" Israel as his people "forever," and then he appeals to the Lord in the second half of the prayer to fulfill his promise to David by "establishing" David's house "forever." The "establishment" of both seems to be intertwined.

An awareness of the Lord's dealings with Israel is crucial to a full appreciation of the Lord's dealings with David. This becomes clearer when we consider our third important theme of David's prayer—his strong acknowledgement of *the incomparability of God*. David places within his three rhetorical questions a double statement about the incomparability of God—"There is none like you, and there is no God besides you" (v. 22). This provides the truth revealed by the three rhetorical questions of amazement. David is amazed that any god would make such a generous promise to him. No one but the God of the Exodus would do such an amazing thing. Just as Moses proclaims the Lord's incomparability in the Song of the Sea, David proclaims new demonstrations of the Lord's divine incomparability in his actions and promises that establish David's house.[10] In both cases it is only because of the Lord's "promise" [Heb. 'word'] and the Lord's "heart" that he does what he does (v. 21). The Lord has done "greatness" for David (v. 21), just as he had done "great and awesome things" for Israel in the Exodus (v. 23).

The themes of king as servant, an appeal for the future grounded in the Lord's deeds in the past, and the incomparability of the Lord are derived solely from the words David prays. The narrator introduces the final important theme of the prayer when he reports that David prays "before the Lord." In this, David assumes *the proper position for prayer*. There is evidence of extensive discussion among the ancient rabbis concerning the verb here (*wayyesheb*—"and he sat/remained before the Lord"). Some rabbis insisted that no one was allowed to "sit" in the central shrine area, and so they translated the verb "remained"; others argued that an exception to the rule against sitting was allowed for the Davidic monarch.[11] It is not necessary to resolve that debate here, because my point concerns the fact that David is "before the Lord." This phrase has figurative implications that go beyond the physical reality of where he is while he prays; these implications are not affected by whether he is sitting or standing at the time. Being cognizant that one is in the Lord's presence during prayer profoundly affects one's attitude and words in prayer, but also how one behaves at all times before and after prayer. The position for prayer that the narrator reports is significant because it points to the deeper spiritual condition of David's heart. This is a condition that is promoted by recognition of the memories that David mentions in this prayer, and it is a condition of his heart that he should strive to maintain as he lives out his life.

Subsequent examples of "before the Lord" in the prayer illuminate its significance and show that the notion extends beyond the act of prayer itself. David prays that the Lord's graciously granted approval be extended to his descendants. He prays that his royal house "will be established before you" (v. 26). He prays the Lord will bless his house, "that it may continue forever before you" (v. 29). David is not speaking here of the physical position of his house relative to the Ark of the Covenant; he is alluding to the Lord's gracious approval and support of David's house, which it is necessary for David's house to receive if the house is to prosper and thrive.

What one does "before the Lord" one does with the greatest respect and humility.[12] "The audience is watching," and that audience is the Lord. As with any person of high status, there are protocols to maintain and manners to watch. David himself is a king, so he understands how these things work. As a king, he would also understand that being "before the Lord" reveals something about the Lord's feelings toward the worshiper. It shows the Lord's gracious approval. David cannot force or demand a seat "before the Lord." The Lord must grant the privilege.[13]

Before turning briefly to two other royal prayers, I would remind us of the four themes I have highlighted in this prayer. David has consolidated ("established") Israel's control of its land, and he has now offered to build a house for the Lord, who has given Israel victory in battle after battle. A house for the Lord should solidify the fact that the Lord now dwells among his people, as he has desired to do for many generations. What David does in his prayer is to model *the proper servant attitude* that all worshipers should have in prayer. This is particularly important for kings, who function as role models for the people. They approach the Lord as individual worshipers and as representatives of the nation they lead. The most powerful individuals in the nation need to realize that the Lord has blessed them, individually and corporately, so that he might dwell in their midst. In some cases, the blessings have come in a historical context of oppression and hardship; in some cases, the blessings have come in a context of prosperity and abundance. The kings and the people, individually and corporately, should develop an attitude of confident humility in any context. David asks that *the Lord's future actions* on behalf of the individual believer *be consistent with* and even further *what he has done for faithful worshipers in the past*. What is more, the Lord's past actions on behalf of his people demonstrate his *incomparability*; no other god does such things. Just as the Lord has kept his promises concerning Israel, David prays that the Lord will keep his promises to David's house (vv. 25–26). It is only because of the Lord's promises to him that David has the courage to pray for what he does (v. 27). It is only by the Lord's blessing that David's house will continue and prosper (v. 29). This gives worshipers courage to ask for the Lord's continuing presence and blessing. But in this there is also a reminder that the relationship is reciprocal, as worshipers should realize that their prayers and their entire lives take place *"before the Lord"* and in response to his actions on their behalf. Their future depends on the workings of the Lord, and so they should adopt the same attitude that David has adopted, the attitude of a servant.

# THE PRAYERS OF SOLOMON AND HEZEKIAH

The second royal prayer reiterates and recasts these four ideas in a slightly different historical context. The Prayer of Solomon, in 1 Kings 8, is set at the dedication of the Jerusalem Temple to the worship of the Lord. Like his father before him, Solomon refers to David and then to himself as *"your servant"* (vv. 24, 25, 26, 28, 29, 30), thus reaffirming the servant attitude that David exuded. He extends this servant designation beyond himself to his descendants and even the entire nation of Israel, moving effortlessly back and forth between "your servants" (vv. 23, 32, 36) and "your people Israel" (vv. 30, 33, 34, 36, 38, 41, 43, 44, 50, 51, 52).

Solomon starts the preamble to his prayer with a reference back to the Lord's command for a place in which he is to dwell (vv. 12–13). Like the first half of David's prayer, the preamble (vv. 12–21) reiterates the Lord's *past dealings*, which sets the tone and the example for Solomon's requests regarding the Lord's *present and future dealings* with the Davidic house and the nation of Israel. The introduction of the main body of the prayer speaks of the Lord's *incomparability*, demonstrated in the Lord's promises to David and his faithful fulfillment of those promises in the life of Solomon (vv. 23–24). Then he turns his attention to the future, asking the Lord to continue to honor his promises to David through David's descendants (vv. 25–26). But the situation has changed slightly since David's day. The physical place of worship now is a permanent structure, reflecting the permanent nature of the Lord's dwelling among his people. The Jerusalem Temple vividly represents what Moses forecasts in the Song of the Sea. The Lord brought his people to the mountain of his inheritance, and now he has firmly established the place he made for his dwelling.

It is intriguing, then, to see where Solomon moves next in his prayer. Rather than pointing to the grandeur of the temple he has built and commenting on its superiority to the preceding tent, Solomon speaks of the inadequacy of the Jerusalem temple—or any earthly temple—to serve as a dwelling place for the Lord. "But will God indeed dwell on the earth? Behold heaven and the highest heaven cannot contain you" (v. 27). What makes this profound theological comment even more intriguing is the next sentence, in which Solomon asks the Lord to hear the prayer "that your servant prays *before you* this day" (v. 28). Solomon is physically positioned, like his father, in a place of worship (he stands "before the altar of the Lord"—v. 22; cf. v. 31). But from this position, Solomon downplays the physical notion of the temple as the Lord's dwelling place, and in so doing he highlights the notion that praying "*before the Lord*" says more about the condition of the worshiper's heart than the position of the worshiper's body. He reinforces this perspective by giving reminders to the people and the kings to "walk before the Lord" with full devotion. He affirms that the Lord "keeps covenant" with those who "walk before you with all their heart" (v. 23). He quotes the Lord's promise to David conditionally, basing its fulfillment on whether David's descendants will *"walk before me* as you [David] have walked before me" (v. 25).[14] As with David's prayer, Solomon's prayer shows that the physical position of the one praying should point to a parallel spiritual condition, because the physical position without the spiritual condition is ultimately meaningless. They do not just "sit" before the Lord in prayer, they "walk" before the Lord every day.

Solomon launches from this statement of orientation into a much longer iteration of future prayers, as he envisions seven situations that might prompt worshipers to pray for deliverance from sin or physical hardship (vv. 27–53). He calls on future petitioners to pray "toward this place/house" (vv. 35, 38, 42, 44, 48; cf. vv. 31, 33), and he calls on the Lord to "open his eyes... toward this temple" (v. 29) and "hear in heaven" (vv. 30, 32, 34, 36, 39, 43, 45, 49) the various prayers that individuals or the nation might pray. The reader should realize by now that, in all these cases, the physical positioning that Solomon describes serves merely as a reminder of the deeper spiritual condition of the heart that the worshiper(s) must exhibit on a daily basis.

The orientation regarding prayer at the Jerusalem Temple helps to interpret the message in the third and final royal prayer, the prayer of Hezekiah (2 Kings 19:14–19). Hezekiah and the city of Jerusalem are under attack by the Assyrian army of Sennacherib (cf. 1 Kings 8:33–34). The king of Assyria sends a letter to Hezekiah, trying to dissuade Hezekiah from putting his faith in the Lord to deliver Jerusalem from the mighty Assyrians. The Assyrian king's primary argument is that Jerusalem's god is no different from the gods of the other nations he has recently conquered. Hezekiah responds in prayer at the Temple, explicitly utilizing two of the four characteristics we have seen in the earlier royal prayers while implicitly being aware of the other two. One implicit feature is the *servant attitude* that is so strongly voiced in the prayers of David and Solomon. Hezekiah exudes the attitude of a servant in his prayer, even though he does not directly refer to himself as "your servant." In fact, he does not refer to himself at all. Perhaps Hezekiah proclaims his servant attitude by his silence about himself. He prays on behalf of the nation ("us"— v. 19) for the Lord to "save" the city. The divine response concludes with a promise to save the city "for the sake of my servant David" (v. 34).

Two of the four previously identified themes are explicit in Hezekiah's prayer. Like David and Solomon before him, the narrator shows Hezekiah to be cognizant of his stance "before the Lord." He spreads out the Assyrian king's letter "before the Lord," and then he prays "before the Lord" (vv. 14–15). Moreover, he begins and ends his prayer with a strong statement about the *incomparability* of the Lord, the one true Creator and living God, who rules over all the kingdoms of the earth (vv. 15 and 19). This is the entire basis for his petition. Finally, there is no explicit reference to God's past deeds as a model for present-future deeds, but Hezekiah does make a strong contrast between the recently exhibited impotence of the gods of other nations and the plea for a display of the incomparable power of the Lord in the present. His language is reminiscent of David's words when David faced the giant, Goliath. Hezekiah and Jerusalem now face a "giant" nation in Assyria. Just as Goliath and the Philistines "mocked ['defied' NIV] the armies of the living God," Sennacherib "has sent [a letter] to mock the living God" (1 Sam. 17:26, 36, 45; 2 Kings 19:4, 16, 22, 23; cf. Pss. 74:10, 18; 89:50–51 [MT. vv. 51–52]). Just as David prayed that all the earth may "know" that there is a God is Israel, so Hezekiah prays that all the earth may "know" that the Lord alone is God (1 Sam. 17:47; 2 Kings 19:19).[15] The reader is expected to recognize the multiple clues that show how Hezekiah's faith in the Lord in the face of Assyrian aggression is founded on the divine acts that the Lord performed generations before in behalf of his faithful ancestor, David.

# THE PRAYER(S) OF HANNAH

The final examples of prayer in the DtrH come from Hannah, a common (non-royal) woman, yet she too exhibits the same four themes in her prayers as the three royal prayers already examined. One can infer from this that she too is a model for how readers are to pray. There are actually two prayers of Hannah recorded in 1 Samuel 1–2. The first is a "vow" (*neder*) and a "petition" for a son that she "makes" (*sha'al*—lit. "asks") to the Lord (1 Sam. 1:11, 17, 27). The second is a prayer of thanksgiving (2:1–10), which she utters after the Lord has answered her petition and she has "lent" her son (*hish'alti / sha'ul*) to the Lord (1:28).

The first prayer (1:11) consists of a single sentence, yet Hannah manages to identify herself in it as "your servant" three times. She acknowledges the Lord as her sovereign, exhibiting the same attitude of humility as the righteous kings who will follow. She utters this short prayer "before the Lord" (1:12; cf. v. 19). When Eli questions her state of mind, she declares, "I have been pouring out my soul before the Lord" (1:15), and when she dedicates her son to the Lord, she says she will bring him to be a priest and "appear in the presence of the Lord" (1:22; cf. 2:18). Her recognition that words and actions are performed "before the Lord" reinforces the attitude of humility and respect she exhibits in the prayer itself, just as one observes with the prayers of David and Solomon and Hezekiah.

The longer Prayer of Hannah (1 Sam. 2:1–10) opens with words of exultation (v. 1) and then praise of the Lord's *incomparability* ("there is none holy like the LORD … there is no rock like our God"—v. 2; cf. Deut. 32:31). The balance of her prayer falls into two parts, much like the Prayer of David. The first part of the main body describes how the Lord's past actions demonstrate his incomparability and sovereignty (vv. 3–8). The Lord reverses the fortunes of human beings, making the poor to be rich and the rich to be poor, strengthening the weak and weakening the strong, and so forth. Such control over the affairs of human beings demonstrates his kingship and gives Hannah the hope and confidence to make the claims about the future that she does in the second part of the prayer's main body. Because the Lord controls the affairs of humanity, Hannah finds the courage (see 2 Sam. 7:27) to declare, "He will guard the feet of his faithful ones . . . he will give strength to his king and exalt the horn of his anointed" (1 Sam. 2:9–10). The success of Israel and her kings will be subject to the sovereignty of the Divine King, a fact which all should acknowledge in their prayers, just as Hannah expresses here.

# CONCLUSION

The prayers of the Deuteronomistic History demonstrate that prayer is fundamentally an act of humble confidence. Those voicing the prayers express their humility by assuming the posture of a servant. This is especially telling in light of the fact that kings speak three of the four lengthier prayers recorded in the DtrH. The proper humility of those who pray derives first from their recognition of the previous deeds that the Lord has graciously performed on their behalf and on behalf of other worshipers, both past and present. Those previous deeds demonstrate the incomparability of the Lord, because the Lord has done what no other has done or could do. Proper humility also derives from the worshipers' recognition that they pray "before the Lord." They demonstrate this recognition in every aspect of their lives, not just in the way they pray. They "walk" before the Lord; there is no difference between the attitude with which they pray and the attitude with which they live their daily lives. As Paul says, they present their bodies—their entire selves—as "a living sacrifice to God" (Rom. 12:1). Their prayers represent just one of many examples of the way they live their lives.

The prayers of the DtrH also reflect unwavering confidence in the Lord. Like the petitioners' humility, this confidence is based on the Lord's incomparability and previous deeds of power, mercifully extended to the faithful. Hannah expresses confidence in divine protection for the faithful, especially the king; David prays confidently for the establishment and sustenance of his dynasty; Solomon prays confidently for forgiveness and relief from suffering in future generations; and Hezekiah prays confidently for deliverance from a seemingly unbeatable foe. Such a perspective on prayer should serve as a guide and inspiration to all readers of these books.

---

1. Samuel Balentine argues that Hebraic "prayer" is part of the fundamentally dialogical nature of the divine-human relationship. It is not merely dichotomous, in which two parties fulfill their respective roles. There is an aspect of reciprocity to the relationship, which prayers exemplify. S. Balentine, *Prayer in the Hebrew Bible: The Drama of Divine-Human Dialogue*, in OBT (Minneapolis: Fortress, 1993), esp. 261–64. The shortcoming in such a definition is that one must then explain how to differentiate prayer from dialogues between God and prophets.

2. Unless otherwise stated, the ESV translation will be used in this essay.

3. The latter expression carries a broader connotation in Chronicles, where it indicates worship or devotion more generally (1 Chr. 21:29–30; 22:19; 28:9; 2 Chr. 12:14; 14:4, 7; 15:2, 12, 13; etc.). Evil kings are those who "inquire of" or "seek" some other god (2 Kings 1:2, 3, 6, 16; 2 Chr. 25:15, 20).

4. A few passages cite prayers of only one or two sentences, giving little more than a summary of the prayer uttered (for example, 1 Kings 18:36–37; 2 Kings 6:17–18; 20:3).

5. Balentine, *Prayer in the Hebrew Bible*, 19–21. Balentine attributes the designation to J. Corvin, "A Stylistic and Functional Study of the Prose Prayers in the Historical Narratives of the Old Testament" (PhD diss., Emory University, 1972).

6. Balentine follows Corvin in excluding Hannah's "prayer" from his list of "formal prayers," and for good reason. Of the five characteristics Corvin identifies for formal prayers, the only one associated with Hannah's prayer is the label, *tepillah*. There is no address to God or to other worshipers, no invocation of God, and no transition to a petition of any sort. Hers is a

"prayer of thanksgiving" about God (P. D. Miller, *They Cried to the Lord; The Form and Theology of Biblical Prayer* [Minneapolis: Augsburg Fortress, 1994], 183–84).

7. Balentine, *Prayer in the Hebrew Bible*, 262.

8. This is the most common translation (KJV, RSV, NASB, NRSV, ESV, NKJV). Other English translations read "Sovereign Lord" (NIV), "Lord Jehovah" (ASV), and "Lord Yahweh" (NJB).

9. For a fuller discussion of this construction, see Timothy M. Willis, "The Curious Case of *kurie mou kurie* in 2 Kingdoms 7:18–29," *JBL* 132, (2013): 515–26.

10. As the people of Israel stand by the Red Sea and look back on the ten plagues and crossing through the Sea, Moses sings the Song of the Sea. He says,

> Who among the gods is like you, O LORD?
> Who is like you—majestic in holiness,
> awesome in glory, working wonders? (Exod. 15:11)

11. One can see some sensitivity to this question in the comments of A. A. Anderson (*2 Samuel*, WBC 11 [Dallas: Word Books, 1989], 126) and P. Kyle McCarter, Jr. (*II Samuel*, AB 9 [New York: Doubleday, 1984], 236). For an extended treatment of the ancient discussion, see Joshua Schwartz, "'To Stand—Perhaps to Sit': Sitting and Standing in the Azarah in the Second Temple Period," in *Sanctity of Time and Space in Tradition and Modernity* (Jewish & Christian Perspectives Series, Vol. 1; ed. by A. Houtman, M. Poorthuis, and J. Schwartz; Leiden: Brill, 1998), 167-89.

12. The preceding dance of David provides a good example of the respectful humility involved in doing something "before the Lord." Michal accuses David of acting shamefully "before the eyes of his servants' maids" (NRSV), but David responds by stating twice that he was dancing "before the Lord" and thus does not mind that he might appear "contemptible" or "abased" in his own eyes (2 Sam. 6:20-22).

13. Donald F. Murray, *Divine Prerogative and Royal Pretension: Pragmatics, Poetics and Polemics in a Narrative Sequence about David (2 Samuel 5.17-7.29)* JSOTSup 264, (Sheffield: Sheffield Academic, 1998), 224–26.

14. This observation suggests that there is an implied conditionality to the unconditional tone of the promise in 2 Samuel 7. The issue of the tone of biblical covenants (conditional or unconditional) is extremely complex. For a treatment that reflects the same perspective as I suggest here—along with extensive bibliography on the issue—see Gray Knoppers, "Ancient Near Eastern Royal Grants and Davidic Covenant: A Parallel?" *JAOS* 116, (1996): 670–697.

15. One might also note the parallel between David's confident assertion before battle ("The LORD, who saved me from the hand of the lion and the hand of the bear, will save me from the hand of this Philistine"—1 Sam. 17:37) and Hezekiah's petition before battle ("O Lord our God, save us from his hand"—2 Kings 19:19). Likewise, Elijah's prayer at Mount Carmel (1 Kings 18:36–37) includes the features of the servant attitude ("I am your servant") and God's incomparability ("that this people may know that you, O LORD, are God"). The other features previously identified can only be inferred.

# Prayer in the Major Prophets (Isaiah, Jeremiah, Ezekiel)

John T. Willis

## Introductory Observations

The books of Isaiah, Jeremiah, and Ezekiel use several words and phrases for prayer.

In some cases, the context indicates the meaning of the word or phrase. In other cases, the phrase reveals its meaning. Sometimes the same word or phrase has different meanings in different contexts. The Hebrew root usually translated "pray" in the Hebrew Bible is *pll*. The verb *hithpallel* appears seven times in Isaiah (16:12; 37:15, 21; 38:2; 44:17; 45:14, 20) and ten times in Jeremiah (7:16; 11:14; 14:11; 29:7, 12; 32:16; 37:3; 42:2, 4, 20). The Hebrew noun *tephillah*, "prayer," occurs five times in Isaiah (1:15; 37:4; 38:5; 56:7 [2x]) and two times in Jeremiah (7:16; 11:14). Prayer is directed "to" Yahweh (Isa. 37:15, 21; 38:2; Jer. 29:7, 12; 32:16; 37:3; 42:2, 4, 20). Thus, anyone who prays assumes Yahweh is near, and a person can talk to Yahweh as he would talk to a fellow human being.

The expression "cry out to Yahweh" (using the Hebrew roots *z'q, s'q, qr', rnn, sw'*) is a petition to Yahweh for help, which appears three times in Isaiah (19:20; 30:19; 58:9), four times in Jeremiah (7:16; 11:11, 14; 14:12), and three times in Ezekiel (8:18; 9:8; 11:13).[1] "Call on [the name of] Yahweh" occurs six times in Isaiah (12:4; 41:25; 43:22; 55:6; 58:9; 65:24) and four times in Jeremiah (3:4; 10:25; 29:12; 33:3) in the sense of petition to Yahweh. The expression to "seek" Yahweh or God means to pray to Yahweh, which appears six times in Isaiah (8:19; 9:13 [MT v. 12]; 31:1; 55:6; 58:2; 65:1), two times in Jeremiah (10:21; 21:2), and seven times in Ezekiel (14:3; 20:1, 3 [2x], 31 [2x]; 36:37). "Seek Yahweh" stands in synonymous parallelism with "call on Yahweh" in Isa 55:6. The Hebrew verb *paga*, "intercede," occurs once in Isaiah (53:12) two times in Jeremiah (7:16; 27:18). The term "entreat the favor of Yahweh" (Hebrew *halal 'eth pene yhwh*) appears in Jeremiah 26:19. One form of the term "make supplication" or "supplication" occurs once in Isaiah (19:22) and three times in Jeremiah (36:7; 42:2, 9).[2]

Prayer is a very broad term that includes several different types, which may be distinguished by the content and intention of the prayer. Prayer includes (1) praise or adoration; (2) confession; (3) thanksgiving; (4) petition, entreaty, or supplication, i.e., asking Yahweh for something that an individual or a group of people wants or needs; (5) intercession; (6) lament or complaint; (7) imprecation or curse.[3]

The Enlightenment has strongly influenced many people to assume that human reason lies at the heart of all life, including religion. Rationalists enjoy making sharp distinctions between categories, most of which are unfounded from a biblical perspective. It would be a very serious mistake to sharply distinguish between a prayer, a prophecy, and a song. Songs, prayers, and prophecies are usually closely connected; it would be impossible to distinguish each one convincingly. The context in each case determines the meaning and significance. For example, 1 Samuel 2:1–10 calls the words of Hannah a "prayer" (v. 1), but this is clearly a poem, a song. Similarly, Mary's praise of God in Luke 1:46–55 begins with the introduction, "And Mary *said*," not *sang, prophesied*, or *prayed*. Yet the content makes clear that this is a prayer of praise, but since it is a poem, one can call this a song. Luke 1:67 calls the poem in Luke 1:68–79 a "prophecy," but it is also a poem or song that could be called a prayer. Matthew 6:9–15 and Luke 11:2–4 entitle the poem of the Lord's Prayer a prayer. Each interpreter must attempt to determine the category of each passage.

A careful study of the Major Prophets elicits actual prayers, texts concerning prayer, and theological ideas concerning prayer in texts in which there may be no direct reference to prayer.

## 1. Prayer in Colloquy or Conversation

One might assume that prayer is a unilateral or one-sided action performed by an individual directed to God. But biblically, prayer involves both a human being and God. "Prayer in the Hebrew Bible," Balentine notes, "is dominated primarily by the never-ending need of believers to maintain some divine-human dialogue in the face of the imbalance between expectation and experience."[4] First, prayer is a human response to what God has already said or done or been involved in some way or another. Then, God responds in a wide variety of ways. After that, human beings often react to God's responses.

God is not a machine, a robot, or an abstract thing, but rather a person. This does not mean that God is a human person; instead, he is an invisible, spiritual being (John 1:18; 1 Tim. 1:17; 6:16). God's actions and reactions are shaped by the circumstances in which he is operating at the time, the people involved in those circumstances, and the effect his actions will have on all involved. God has *idealistic* short-range and long-range plans involving human beings, but he deals with each situation *idealistically* in light of his or her situation spiritually, intellectually, emotionally, socially and every other way. *Idealistically*, God is "not wanting *any* to perish, but *all* to come to repentance" (2 Pet. 3:9; cf. Rom. 2:4). But *realistically*, many people refuse to repent because of their hard and impenitent hearts, and consequently, God pours out his "wrath and fury" on them (Rom. 2:5–9).

Isaiah and Jeremiah emphasize that prayer involves a dialogue between believers or worshippers and Yahweh. Isaiah 30:18–19 contains Yahweh's promise to Zion:

Therefore the LORD *waits to be gracious* for you;

Therefore he will rise up to *show mercy* to you.

For the LORD is a God of justice;

blessed are all those who wait for him.

Truly, O people of Zion, inhabitants of Jerusalem, you shall weep no more. He will surely be gracious to you at the sound of *your cry*; when he *hears* it, he will *answer* you.[5]

Isaiah 56:6–7 presents an astounding announcement of Yahweh's powerful work:

And the foreigners who join themselves to the LORD.
>    to minister to him, to love the name of the LORD,
>    and to be his servants;
> all who keep the sabbath, and do not profane it,
>    and hold fast my covenant—
> these I will bring to my holy mountain
>    and make them joyful in *my house of prayer*,
> their burnt offerings and their sacrifices
>    will be accepted on my altar;
> for *my house shall be called a house of prayer*
>    for all peoples.

This announcement has strong affinities with Solomon's prayer at the dedication of the Jerusalem temple in 1 Kings 8:27–53, (especially vv. 41–43), "when a foreigner, who is not from your people Israel, comes from a distant land because of your [Yahweh's] name—for they shall hear of your great name, your mighty hand, and your outstretched arm— when a foreigner comes and *prays* toward this house, then *hear in heaven your dwelling place*, and do according to all that the foreigner calls to you, so that all the peoples of the earth may know your name and fear you, as do our people Israel."[6]

Isaiah 65 emphasizes Yahweh's strong desire to establish and maintain an ongoing relationship with all people. A few lines bring out this important concept, as Yahweh declares:

> I was *ready to be sought out* by those who did not *ask*,
>    to *be found* by those who did not *seek* me.
> I said, 'Here I am, here I am,'
>    to a nation that did not *call on my name*.
> *I held out my hands* all day long
>    to a rebellious people,
> who walk in a way that is not good,
>    following their own devices. (vv.1-2)

> For I am about to create new heavens
>    and a new earth;
> the former things shall not be remembered
>    or come to mind. (v.17)

Before they *call* I will answer,
while they *are yet speaking* I will *hear*. (v. 24)

## 2. Prayer as a Collective or Communal Activity

Prayer is not an isolated individual activity, but a part of ongoing godly living shared with the community of faith. Acceptable prayer is God-centered and other-centered, not egocentric. In an oracle concerning Moab, Yahweh through the prophet declares,

We have heard of the *pride* of Moab
—how *proud* he is!—
of his arrogance, his *pride*, and his *insolence*;
his *boasts* are false. (Isa. 16:6)

The prophet continues later in the oracle, "When Moab presents himself, when he wearies himself upon the high place, when he comes to his sanctuary to *pray*, he will not prevail" (16:12).

Isaiah 1:10–17 contains an oracle denouncing regular worshippers who bring their sacrifices, their festivals, and their prayers but refuse to help the needy, the poor, the widow, and the orphan. Note especially verses 15–17.

When you stretch out your hands,
I will hide my eyes from you;
even though you *make many prayers*,
I will not listen;
your hands are full of blood.
Wash yourselves; make yourselves clean;
remove the evil of your doings
from before my eyes;
cease to do evil,
learn to do good
seek justice,
rescue the oppressed,
defend the orphan,
plead for the widow.

## 3. Diversity in Prayer

Different types of prayer appear throughout the prophetic material.

### a. Praise or Adoration

Isaiah addresses his audience at Jerusalem in worship:

> Sing praises to the LORD, for he has done gloriously;
>> Let this be known in all the earth.
> Shout aloud and sing for joy, O royal Zion,
>> for great in your midst is the Holy One of Israel."
>> (Isa. 12:5–6)

The prophet praises Yahweh for delivering his people from oppression from his enemies:

> O LORD, you are my God;
>> I will exalt you, I will praise your name;
> for you have done wonderful things,
> plans formed of old, faithful and true. (Isa. 25:1)

Encouraging the Judean exiles in Babylonian, the anonymous prophet proclaims:

> Sing to the LORD a new song,
>> his praise from the ends of the earth!
> Let the sea roar and all that fills it,
>> the coastlands and their inhabitants.
> Let the desert and its towns lift up their voice,
>> the villages that Kedar inhabits;
> let the inhabitants of Sela sing for joy,
>> let them shout from the tops of the mountains.
> Let them give glory to the LORD,
> and declare his praise in the coastlands. (Isa. 42:10–12; cf.
>> Jer. 20:13)

In a similar situation, Jeremiah encourages the Judean exiles:

> For thus says the LORD:
> Sing aloud with gladness for Jacob,
>> and raise shouts for the chiefs of the nations;
> proclaim, give praise, and say,

"Save, O LORD, your people,
the remnant of Israel." (Jer. 31:7)

Indirect references to praising Yahweh appear in Isaiah 62:8–9, 64:11.

### b. Confession

In the vision call of Isaiah, after the prophet realizes he is in the presence of the King of the universe, the Lord of hosts, he falls on his knees and proclaims, "Woe is me! I am lost, for I am a man of unclean lips, and I live among a people of unclean lips; yet my eyes have seen the King, the LORD of hosts!" (Isa. 6:5)

### c. Thanksgiving

After having been through a period of discipline, Isaiah announced:
You will say in that day:
I will give thanks to you, O LORD,
for though you were angry with me,
your anger turned away, and you comforted me...

And you will say in that day:
Give thanks to the LORD,
call on his name;
make known his deeds among the nations;
proclaim that his name is exalted" (Isa. 12:1, 4).

One of the hope oracles in Jeremiah announces that in the waste and desolate cities and towns of Judah:
There shall once more be heard the voice of mirth and the voice of gladness, the voice of the bridegroom and the voice of the bride, the voices of those who sing, as they bring thank offerings to the house of the LORD:

"Give thanks to the LORD of hosts,
for the LORD is good,
for his steadfast love endures forever!"
For I will restore the fortunes of the land as at first, says the LORD. (Jer. 33:10–11)

Further indirect allusions to thanksgiving appear in Isaiah 51:3 and Jeremiah 30:19.

### d. Petition, Entreaty, Supplication

The Book of Isaiah narrates two significant events in which King Hezekiah of Judah fervently approached Yahweh in prayer for help. In the first few years of Hezekiah's reign, Yahweh sent the prophet Isaiah to tell Hezekiah that he would die very soon. After Isaiah left,

> Hezekiah turned his face to the wall, and *prayed to the* LORD: "Remember now, O LORD, I *implore* you how I have walked before you in faithfulness with a whole heart and have done what is right in your sight." And Hezekiah wept bitterly. Then the word of the LORD came to Isaiah: "Go and say to Hezekiah, Thus says the LORD, the God of your ancestor David: *I have heard your prayer*, I have seen your tears; I will add fifteen years to your life." (Isa 38:1–5; cf. 2 Kings 20:1–7; 2 Chron. 32:24)

Then Hezekiah composed a prayer of gratitude in poetry to Yahweh for having healed him from his illness. Four aspects of this prayer are worthy of consideration. First, Hezekiah begins by describing how he felt when he became ill and was told he would die soon. He did not believe it was fair for him to have to die in the middle of his life before he reached old age, and he believed Yahweh is the one who had cut him off (Isa. 38:10–15). Second, in this situation, Hezekiah cried out desperately to Yahweh to restore him to health (Isa. 38:13a, 14b–c, 16). Third, Hezekiah confessed that Yahweh was justified in smiting him with illness, because he had sinned against God. His illness was for his own good; it was designed to jolt him to his senses, and to bring him to repentance. Hezekiah repented, and now Yahweh has forgiven him of all his sins, and thus has removed the illness (Isa. 38:17–19). Fourth and finally, Hezekiah turned to the future with the assurance that Yahweh will save him, and promises to sing praises to Yahweh all the days of his life (Isa. 38:20). Gene M. Tucker addresses this issue. He reasons:

> Everyone knows that what happens in history and nature is not entirely caused by human actions. Weather is a good example of forces beyond human control. . . . Is everything that happens in the universe fully rational, and human beings just do not know enough yet? . . . Contemporary readers will need to discern the activity, and perhaps even the intervention, of God in their world. . . . Even the prophet [Isaiah] used "medicine" [a

fig poultice—Isa 38:21]. Healing is no less a miracle when the work of medical science and competent professionals than when it comes as a word directly from heaven.[7]

The setting for the second event is when Sennacherib and the Assyrians invaded Judah and destroyed the forty-six fortified cities of Judah in 701 BCE. Then they surrounded or besieged Jerusalem, and shortly later the commander of the Assyrian army, the Rabshakeh, sent a threatening letter to Hezekiah that he and Judah must surrender or the Assyrians will destroy the city (Isa. 36; 2 Kings 18:13–37; 2 Chron. 32:1–19). When Hezekiah received this message, he tore his clothes, covered himself with sackcloth, went to the house of the Lord, and sent a message to Isaiah for consultation. Isaiah responded telling him not to fear because Yahweh will deliver the city (Isa. 37:1–13). Hezekiah then took the letter to the temple, spread it out before the Lord, and composed a moving prayer to petition Yahweh to deliver God's people in this difficult situation. The statement that Hezekiah spread Sennacherib's letter "before the LORD" (v. 14) means that Hezekiah sat (stood, knelt) before the Ark of the Covenant at the Jerusalem temple (for this common practice, see 2 Sam. 7:18) as a symbol of Yahweh's presence as king (see 1 Sam. 4:3–4; 2 Sam. 6:2) to present his petitions to Yahweh.[8]

This prayer consists of four sequential parts. First, Hezekiah extols Yahweh as Lord of hosts, who is enthroned on/between/over the cherubim, who is the only God of all the kingdoms of the earth, maker of heaven and earth (Isa. 37:16). Second, he beseeches Yahweh to incline his ear and hear, open his eyes and see, and hear all the words of Sennacherib which he sent to mock the Living God (Isa. 37:17). Third, Hezekiah reports to Yahweh that the kings of Assyria have laid waste all the nations and hurled their gods into the fire so they were destroyed (Isa. 37:18–19). Fourth and finally, Hezekiah addresses Yahweh directly, imploring him to save the Judeans from the Assyrians so that all the kingdoms of the earth may know that Yahweh alone is God (Isa. 37:20). Yahweh responded by telling Hezekiah that all this was Yahweh's plan all along, and since Hezekiah has prayed fervently, Yahweh will turn back the arrogance of the Assyrians on the way by which they came. An angel of Yahweh struck down 185,000 Assyrian soldiers around Jerusalem, and Sennacherib and the rest of his army left and returned to Nineveh. Later, two of his sons killed him with the sword (Isa. 37:21–38).[9]

Just before the fall of Jerusalem in 587 BCE, Yahweh told Jeremiah to buy a field at his home town of Anathoth from his cousin Hanamel. Jeremiah did this; then Yahweh told him to put the sealed deed of this purchase in an earthenware jar and promises that houses and fields and vineyards will be bought in this land (Jer. 32:1–15). After Jeremiah bought this field, he prayed fervently to Yahweh that Yahweh would eventually bring his faithful people back into the land. This prayer falls into three parts. First, Jeremiah exalts Yahweh above everything else:

- Yahweh made heaven and earth, declaring: "Nothing is too hard for you."
- Yahweh shows steadfast love to the thousandth generation but repaying the guilt of parents into the laps of their children.
- Yahweh is great in counsel and mighty in deeds.
- Yahweh's eyes are open to *all* the ways of mortals, rewarding all according to their ways and the fruit of their doings (Jer. 32:16–19)

Second, Jeremiah briefly summarizes Yahweh's mighty deeds in the past: Yahweh delivered the Israelites out of Egyptian bondage and gave them the land of Canaan, but they did not obey his voice and follow his law, and this is why Yahweh is making all these disasters upon them (Jer. 32:20–23). Third, Jeremiah describes the present situation: the Babylonians have surrounded or besieged Jerusalem and are fighting against the city, but Yahweh told Jeremiah to buy the field at Anathoth knowing all the while that Yahweh has decreed that the Babylonians will take the city and carry the Judeans into exile (Jer. 32:24–25). Yahweh responds by assuring Jeremiah that Yahweh has given Jerusalem into the hand of the Babylonians. But after the exile, Yahweh will gather his scattered people to live in Jerusalem and Judah to rebuild the temple, restore the Law of Moses, and rebuild the wall of the city. Yahweh will give this remnant, restored people an "everlasting covenant," a steadfast marital relationship, giving them one heart and one way that they may fear Yahweh and plant them in faithfulness; indeed, Jeremiah's purchase of the field at Anathoth is a symbol that fields will indeed be bought in this land (Jer. 32:26–44).

## e. Intercession

Intercession is a prayer, petition, or entreaty in behalf of others, and examples of the prophets praying for others include: Samuel (1 Sam. 12:23), Amos (Amos 7:1–6), and Jeremiah (Jer. 18:20). In his letter to the exiles carried into Babylon under Jehoiachin in 598 BCE, Jeremiah reports that Yahweh instructed the people: 1) to stay in Babylon for seventy years and 2) they were to "seek the welfare of the city where I have sent you into exile, and pray to the LORD on its behalf, for in its welfare you will find your welfare." (Jer. 29:4-7) Some of the Jews left in the land of Palestine after the destruction of Jerusalem asked Jeremiah to pray for them that Yahweh would show them the way they should go, and Jeremiah assured them that he would do pray in their behalf (Jer. 42:1–4). Jeremiah 15:1 states that Moses and Samuel stood before God's people, but Yahweh would not turn toward them because of their hard-hearted spirit. On at least three separate occasions, Yahweh specifically commanded Jeremiah not to pray for God's people because of their obstinate, hard-hearted spirit and life. When Jeremiah proclaimed his sermon at the Jerusalem temple about the temple, Yahweh then said to the prophet: "As for you, do not pray for this people, do not raise a cry or prayer on their behalf, and do not intercede with me, for I will not hear you." (Jer. 7:16; cf. Jer. 11:14; 14:11–12)

Ezekiel 9 describes Yahweh choosing six executioners to kill all the young men, young women, little children, and women in Jerusalem except those who had received a mark on their forehead from the man clothed in linen. While they were killing, Ezekiel was left alone; he fell prostrate on his face and cried out: "Ah Lord GOD! Will you destroy all who remain of Israel as you pour out your wrath on Jerusalem?" (Ezek. 9:8) When confronted with the twenty-five men at the entrance of the gateway in Jerusalem, Ezekiel declares that Jerusalem will fall to the Babylonians. While he was prophesying, Pelatiah died. Then Ezekiel fell on his face, cried with a loud voice, and said: "Ah Lord GOD! will you make a full end of the remnant of Israel?" (Ezek. 11:13)

## f. Lament or Complaint

The prophet Jeremiah often felt that Yahweh had abandoned him, and had not supported Jeremiah when Yahweh had assured him that he would. So, Jeremiah often approaches Yahweh in prayer with various types of complaints or laments. All of these appear in Jeremiah 11–20. There are at least six complaints of Jeremiah in this book.

In one prayer, Yahweh responded by honoring Jeremiah's complaint. Jeremiah declares:

> It was the LORD who made it known to me, and I knew;
>> then you showed me their evil deeds.
> But I was like a gentle lamb
>> led to the slaughter.
> And I did not know it was against me
>> that they devised schemes, saying,
> "Let us destroy the tree with its fruit,
>> let us cut him off from the land of the living,
>> so that his name will no longer be remembered!'
> But you, O LORD of hosts, who judge righteously,
>> who try the heart and the mind,
> let me see your retribution upon them,
>> for to you I have committed my cause. (Jer. 11:18–20)

Yahweh responded by stating: "I am going to punish them; the young men shall die by the sword, their sons and their daughters shall die by famine; and not even a remnant shall be left of them. For I will bring disaster upon the people of Anathoth, the year of their punishment." (11:22–23)

Patrick D. Miller presents a masterful exegesis of this text. He emphasizes that Jeremiah is unaware of the plots of his enemies "as he depicts himself as an innocent lamb led to slaughter, going about his business quite unaware that the butchers are ready to cut his throat." Such thinking and language is typical of lament prayers (cf. Ps. 44:11 [MT 44:12]). Common features of lament prayers are schemes and plots of enemies (see Pss. 7:14, 10:2, 35:4, 36:4, 140:2), quotations of the enemy's intent (see Pss. 2:3, 12:4, 35:25, 71:11), and approbations of Yahweh's nature as "you who judge righteously" (Jer. 11:20; see Pss. 7:11, 9:4). Miller observes, "Prayer involves the laying out of a case before God on the assumption that God will assess and act appropriately." Praying people attempt to motivate and arouse God to act against wicked people and defend those who attempt to serve him.[10] Additional complaint prayers of Jeremiah appear in Jer. 15:15–20, 17:14–18, 18:18–23, 20:7–18.

Ezekiel 18 contains Yahweh's response to the popular proverb: "The parents have eaten sour grapes, and the children's teeth are set on edge," meaning that a child is responsible for the sins of his or her parents. Yahweh declares that each person is responsible for his or her own sins, not for the sins of the parents, presenting an elaborate description of each righteous person and each rebellious person (Ezek. 18:1–18). The people respond in prayer offering two objections: (1) Why should not the son suffer for the iniquity of the father? (Ezek. 18:19), and (2) The way of the Lord is unfair (Ezek. 18:25, 29). Yahweh replies by insisting that *his way* is not unfair, but righteous, while the way of his people is unjust because they suffer because of their own sins (Ezek. 18:19–32).

### g. Imprecation or Curse

Jeremiah utters imprecations or curses against his enemies in his complaint or lament prayers. In Jeremiah's first lament, the prophet says that Yahweh made known to him the evil plans of his enemies to destroy him which Jeremiah would not have known otherwise. These enemies are his friends in his hometown of Anathoth (Jer. 11:18–19, 21). Jeremiah responds by extolling Yahweh as the Lord of hosts who judges righteously, who tries the heart and the mind, and by making this request to Yahweh: "Let me see your retribution upon them [Jeremiah's enemies], for to you I have committed my cause" (Jer 11:20). Yahweh responds by assuring Jeremiah that He will honor his request to punish Jeremiah's enemies, who shall die by the sword and famine and none of them shall be left, for Yahweh will bring disaster on the people of Anathoth (Jer. 11:22–23). Similar imprecations texts appear in Jeremiah 12:3c–d, 15:15, 17:18, 18:21–23, 20:12.

Many people are troubled or offended by such clear biblical imprecations or curses. Some argue that such prayers contradict the instructions of Jesus in the Sermon on the Mount, "Love your enemies and pray for those who persecute you" (Matt. 5:44), and, thus, could not possibly be appropriate for Christians. But the New Testament contains numerous imprecations by Jesus (Matt. 25:41), Peter (Acts 1:20), Paul (Acts 13:10–11; 23:1–5; 2 Thess. 1:8; Gal. 1:8–9; Rom. 12:17–21; 1 Cor. 16:22), and John (Rev. 6:9–10).

# THEOLOGICAL INSIGHTS ABOUT PRAYER FROM THE MAJOR PROPHETS

Prayer is not an academic subject to be discussed or debated, nor a spiritual exercise or an act of worship designed to make the worshipper feel good, nor an existential experience in which a person communes with himself in the quietness of his own solitude. Rather it is a person's conversation with a living personality, God, a natural response to God's prior down reach to humanity through nature, his mighty works, and his revelation of himself and his will in his word. The privilege of prayer is due to God's grace. No one is worthy to pray (Rom. 3:23). Isaiah acknowledged this reality (Isa. 6:5). In spite of this, Yahweh is anxious to hear and answer prayers (Isa. 65:24).

## 1. God encourages people to speak their minds

Yahweh specifically denounces his people when they honor him with their mouths and lips, but their hearts are far from him (Isa. 29:13–14; cf. Titus 1:16). The kind of people whose prayers are acceptable to God are genuine, honest, and true. There is no one perfect way in which one must feel when she/he prays to God, but God wants the worshipper to be honest before God.

W. L. Liefeld observes: "The inclusion of Jeremiah's outburst of frustration (20:7–18) in the canonical scriptures is an encouragement to honesty with God."[11]

This does not mean that God is pleased with every attitude and petition and expression of thanksgiving which praying people bring to him. Yahweh rebuked Jeremiah for his lament prayer (Jer. 15:15–21). But when people honestly express their feelings to God in prayer, God is in a position to deal with them realistically and meaningfully. Honesty opens the door for further communication with God.

## 2. God Answers Prayer in a Wide Variety of Ways

Since each situation is different, God acts in different ways. God always acts according to his will. As the psalmist says, "Our God is in the heavens; he does whatever he pleases" (Ps. 115:3, cf. Ps 135:6). But God also acts with a view to the effects his actions will have on *all* who will be impacted by his actions. Since human beings can see only a tiny portion of what takes place on earth at any time, and since they have no way of comprehending God's overall plan and purpose of any point in history, it is impossible for people to know what God should do in any situation. It is presumptuous for them to question or doubt that he is carrying out the best thing or the right thing. God may answer prayers in the following ways.

First, God may grant the request of the petitioner. Two good examples of this are the prayers of Hezekiah that Yahweh deliver him from his illness and that Yahweh deliver Jerusalem from the Assyrian invasion under Sennacherib in 701 BCE (Isa. 36–39). In the hope oracles in Ezekiel, Yahweh declares: "I will let the house of Israel ask me to increase their population like a flock." (Ezek. 36:37)

Second, God may reject the request of the petitioner because it is self-centered or because this is not best for the person involved or because God has a better or different purpose in mind. Yahweh sternly denounced Jeremiah because of his lament prayer in Jeremiah 15:15–18 because Jeremiah was too concerned about his own discomfort and accused Yahweh of being dishonest, comparing Yahweh with "a deceitful brook," "waters that fail." (Jer. 15:18) Yahweh responded that Jeremiah must repent (Jer. 15:19–21). Yahweh told Ezekiel that though God's people in Jerusalem cry in Yahweh's hearing with a loud voice, Yahweh will not listen to them because their hearts are hardened (Ezek. 8:18). Yahweh instructed Ezekiel concerning certain elders of Israel who came and sat before the prophet: "These men have taken their idols into their hearts, and placed their iniquity as a stumbling block before them; shall I let myself be consulted by them?" (Ezek. 14:3); the obvious answer is NO! See also Ezek. 20:1, 3, 31; 1 John 5:14).

Third, God gives the petitioner something better than he/she asks. In Jeremiah's prayer in Jeremiah 32:17, he says: "Ah Lord GOD! It is you who made the heavens and the earth by your great power and your outstretched arm! Nothing is too hard for you" (cf. Gen. 18:12–14; 2 Cor. 12:7–10).

## 3. God Exposes the Difference between Sincere and Self-Seeking Prayer

In the contexts of the books of Isaiah, Jeremiah, and Ezekiel, God's people faithfully attended public assemblies and worship activities. Yahweh's true prophets were among the attendees. But on several occasions, Yahweh motivated a prophet to denounce the worshippers because their worship is insincere. A dialogue between Yahweh and Israel appears in Jeremiah 3:21–4:4. Yahweh begins by inviting his hearers: "Return, O faithless children, I will heal your faithlessness" (Jer. 3:21–22a). The hearers respond:

Here we come to you;

for you are the LORD our God…

Let us lie down in our shame, and let our dishonor cover us; for we have sinned against the LORD our God, we and our ancestors, from our youth even to this day; and we have no obeyed the voice of the LORD our God (Jer. 3:22b, 25).

This appears to be a sincere prayer of penitence. But Yahweh sees through the hypocrisy, and replies:

If you return, O Israel,

says the LORD,

if you return to me;

if you remove your abominations from my presence,

and do not waver,

and if you swear, "As the LORD lives!"

in truth, in justice, and in righteousness,

then nations shall be blessed by him,

and by him they shall boast (Jer. 4:1–2).

Isaiah addresses the people of Jerusalem as "the rulers of Sodom" and "the people of Gomorrah." They bring numerous animal sacrifices, incense, new moon, Sabbath, and appointed festivals. Yahweh's response is that he hates such behavior (Isa. 1:10–17).

# PRAYER IN THE LIFE OF INDIVIDUALS, THE CHURCH, AND THE NATION BASED ON THE MAJOR PROPHETS

Biblical speakers and writers assume that God has personal characteristics and is deeply concerned with the well-being of human beings individually and collectively in ongoing relationships. It is true that God is transcendent, but he is also immanent universally and individually. The God we serve is anxious to hear and respond through words, actions, or both in keeping with his own will to carry out his overall purpose for the world. While God is mysterious, from time to time he reveals glimpses of his nature in nature, history, and his revealed word.

When we pray, we are attempting to communicate with God. God has already spoken through his chosen spokespersons and through his mighty deeds in history, and we naturally respond to his words and works, and as fresh needs and problems and concepts enter into our lives, we seek God's help and guidance. As Liefeld reminds us, "Prayer is a response to multiple explicit and implicit invitations of God."[12] God does not seek prayer from only the elite, the wise, the prophet, the priest, the elder, the preacher, the religious teacher, the saint, the ascetic, or the cloistered; instead, God encourages all human beings to communicate with him directly and openly.[13]

Any individual, who really believes that God exists and is alive and at work in the world he created, can engage in an ongoing dialogue with his/her creator, and this conversation is as natural as talking with another human being. Prayer is as essential to a full and meaningful life as breathing oxygen or eating food. Human beings are created in the image of God, and thus are fashioned by their very nature to communicate with God. Praying is an acknowledgment that God is sovereign in the universe and in the lives of nations and individuals and that we are totally dependent on God for sustenance, protection, strength, and the fulfillment and accomplishment of abiding purposes and goals in life. Anyone who prays to God turns over their cares, ambitions, and reservations and removes from their shoulders the necessity of achieving wants or needs by their own power.

---

1. Note that in Pss 17:1; 39:12; 61:1, "pray" and "cry out" stand in synonymous parallelism. All citations and quotations from the Bible are according to the NRSV.

2. For further discussion on these terms, see D. R. Ap-Thomas, "Notes on Some Terms relating to Prayer," VT 6 (1956): 230–39; Sheldon H. Blank, "Some Observations concerning Biblical Prayer," Hebrew Union College Annual 32 (1961): 82–87; W. L. Liefeld, "Prayer," in ISBE Fully Revised 3, ed. James Orr (Grand Rapids: Eerdmans, 1986), 931.

3. Elizabeth Achtemeier poignantly observes: "No motif more adequately reveals the nature of biblical faith than does gratitude or thanksgiving . . . It occurs only in the context of the covenant relationship. And it is always prompted by a concrete act of the covenant God within history." Achtemeier, "Gratitude," IDB 2 (1962), 470.

4. Samuel E. Balentine, Prayer in the Hebrew Bible. The Drama of Divine-Human Dialogue, OBT (Minneapolis: Fortress, 1993), 9.

5. In this and subsequent quotations of biblical texts, italics are added to emphasize words or concepts.

6. See further the comments by R. N. Whybray, *Isaiah 40-66*, NCB (London: Oliphants, 1975), 199; Balentine, *Prayer in the Hebrew Bible*, 80-88.

7. Gene M. Tucker, "The Book of Isaiah 1-39: Introduction, Commentary, and Reflections," in *NIB* 6, ed. Leander Keck (Nashville: Abingdon, 2011), 302.

8. Tucker, "The Book of Isaiah 1-39," 294.

9. For important insights, see Balentine, *Prayer in the Hebrew Bible*, 61-64, 91-97.

10. Patrick D. Miller, "The Book of Jeremiah: Introduction, Commentary, and Reflections," *NIB* 6 (Nashville: Abingdon, 2001), 673-75.

11. Liefeld, "Prayer," 933.

12. Liefeld, "Prayer," 937.

13. For further study, see Liefeld, "Prayer," 931-39; H.-P. Stahli, "*pll* to pray," *TLOT* 2, eds. Ernst Jenni and Claus Westermann; trans. Mark E. Biddle; (Peabody, Massachusetts: Hendrickson, 1997), 991-94; Erhard Gerstenberger, "*pll*," in *TDOT* 11 (2001) 567-77; Newman, "Prayer," 579-82.

# Prayer in the Minor Prophets (The Book of the Twelve)

Andrew E. Hill

## Minor Prophets and the Book of the Twelve

The title, "Book of the Twelve," is a Hebrew designation for the books commonly known as the Minor Prophets (cf. Sir. 49:10). Jewish tradition, based upon the interpretive approach known as *midrash halakah* (i.e. story-telling exegesis), assumed the collection of Twelve Prophets was arranged to tell a particular "story" about Israel. Scholars have proposed several unifying themes for the book of the Twelve.[1]

Given Jewish tradition, it seems appropriate to regard the Twelve Prophets as a scroll or "book" loosely unified by the prophetic genre, perhaps with an implied narrative or, narratives structure, and a central theme, or themes. The Twelve Prophets are framed by the prophetic call to repentance, in certain instances employing similar phraseology. Notably, the first two books (Hos. 6:1, 7:10, 14:1–2; Joel 2:12–14) and the last two books of the collection (Zech. 1:3–4; Mal. 3:7) admonish the Hebrews to return to God and restore faithful covenant relationship with him.[2] This theme or emphasis may be instructive for a theology of prayer in the Twelve Prophets, since according to Seitz, prayer has the capacity to reveal God's double-edged life with Israel—his love and commitment and his jealousy prompting judgment.[3]

The theme of *missio Dei* may be another unifying feature of the Twelve Prophets. Recently, Jerry Hwang demonstrated the value of applying the theme of *missio Dei* as an integrative motif in the book of Jeremiah. For Hwang the *missio Dei* is "the sending activity of God with the purpose of reconciling to himself and bringing into his kingdom fallen men and women from every people, nation, and tongue."[4]

The OT prophets generally are involved in the "sending activity" of God and their message is essentially one that calls their audiences to return or to be reconciled to God. Granted this ministry of reconciliation is directed primarily to restoring the nation of Israel in covenant relationship with the LORD. Yet, the OT prophets also had a mission to the nations, albeit a more indirect ministry. In addition to oracles of judgment against the nations found in the Twelve (e.g. Hosea, Joel, Obadiah, Nahum, Habakkuk, Zephaniah), there are also oracles of healing and restoration for the nations, and the worship of God by the nations (Amos 9:11–12; Mic. 4:2–4; Zech. 14:16–19).

Finally, it is worth noting that three, perhaps four books of the Twelve, make reference to the ancient Israelite confession emerging from the LORD's autobiographical declaration in Exodus 34:6–7. Joseph Kelly designates this as the "YHWH creed," a relatively stable formula of God's essential nature and character.[5] The passage is cited (with some variation) in Nahum 1:3, Joel 2:13 and Jonah 4:2. It is possible that Joel 3:21 [MT 4:21] and Micah 7:18–20 allude to the "YHWH creed" as well. This divine testimony has direct implications for prophetic ministry in the book of Jonah and for penitential prayer in the book of Joel since it reveals the essential character of YHWH. Beyond this, it may have subtle implications for prayer more broadly in the Twelve since this formula describes the LORD's basic character and informs Hebrew sensibilities related to repentance and return to God, intercessory prayers, and petitions offered to the LORD of the Sinai covenant.

# DEFINITION OF PRAYER

A working definition of prayer is essential to any study of biblical prayer. Balentine understands prayer most simply as "explicit communication with God."[6] Patrick Miller describes prayer as "one of the primary modes of relating the divine and the human."[7] While he does not offer a formal definition of prayer, Miller does consider prayer a human-divine dialogue or "conversation with God."[8] In each case, the definition of biblical prayer assumes God is accessible by such means.

The definition of biblical prayer as communication with God or human-divine dialogue will suffice for this study. Unlike Balentine, I would add other forms of prayer on the basis of this definition like the vow, the curse, and oracle seeking (including lot casting).[9] Meditation is another activity that has merit as a form of communication with God and hence is a category of prayer as well. This is especially the case for meditation on the Torah (Ps. 1:2), God's unfailing love (Ps. 48:9), and God's mighty deeds of creation and redemption (Pss. 77:12; 111:2). Lastly, some consideration must also be given to waiting on God in silence as another form of prayer in the OT (cf. Hab. 2:1).

# DELINEATION OF PRAYER FORMS

Identifying biblical prayer texts poses a challenge because one may understand prayer more narrowly as "recorded prayers, texts that preserve the actual words of a prayer."[10] The other end of the spectrum is marked by what Lockyer calls "sidelights" to prayer, texts that support the act of prayer in some fashion (e.g., mood, tone, posture, setting, ethics).[11] The middle ground between "recorded prayers" and "prayer sidelights" includes reports of prayers, and texts that indicate, suggest or imply that prayer has been offered or texts that reference God's hearing (or refusal) to hear prayer. These reports typically are characterized by the use of certain terminology, "code words" signifying prayer activity of some sort, including: "ask" (sha'al), "seek, inquire" (baqash; darash), "cry out" (qara), "entreat" (khala). This study will cast the net widely and include all four prayer forms: recorded prayers, reported prayers, implied reports of prayer, and prayer sidelights. In addition, this analysis will include other channels of divine—human communication as prayer texts where appropriate, namely: the taking of vows, seeking oracles (including lot casting), the curse, and meditation.

# CATEGORIES OF PRAYER

The lists of OT prayer types from Balentine, Miller, and Peskett have been conflated to create a representative taxonomy of prayer forms in the Twelve Prophets.[12] Naturally there will be some ambiguity in classifying particular prayers given the overlap in the categories of prayer forms. Such taxonomies also raise questions related to spontaneous prayers over against prescribed prayers. Greenberg's argument for less rigid distinctions between the two, given "the mixture of spontaneity and prescription in all social behavior," has merit.[13] The relationship of the individual pray-er to the praying community also becomes a point of discussion in the categorization of biblical prayers. Seitz's observation that in Israel's covenant relationship with the LORD "a dialectic exists between the prayer of Everyman and the prayer of the one man" may be helpful on this point.[14] The constraints of this forum prohibit any detailed discussion of these and related questions generated by the taxonomy of prayer types.

# DISTRIBUTION OF PRAYERS IN THE TWELVE PROPHETS BY TYPE

The prayer texts of the Twelve Prophets are identified below according to category.

## 1. Prayers of praise (hymn, doxology, trust, thanksgiving)

Jonah 2:2–9, recorded psalmic prayer of thanksgiving

Hab. 3:1–19, recorded psalmic prayer of thanksgiving and trust

Mal. 1:11, implied prayers of praise with reference to incense offerings

Mal. 1:14, implied prayers of adoration and worship in the "name of the LORD" being reverenced among the nations (also prayers of invocation/benediction?)

Mal. 3:10, implied prayers of thanksgiving with the tithe offerings

## 2. Prayers of confession and penitence (including lamentation and mourning)

Hosea 5:15, implied prayers of penitence when the people seek God in their misery

Hosea 10:12, implied prayers of repentance in the summons to "seek the LORD"

Hosea 14:2–3, recorded prayer of confession

Joel, 1:13, call to raise a prayer of lamentation

Joel 2:12–17, call to fasting and prayers of repentance

Amos 5:4–5, 6, implied prayers of repentance in the call to "seek the LORD"

Jonah 3:8–9, report of prayer of repentance

Zeph. 2:3, implied prayers of repentance in the call to "seek the LORD"

Zeph. 3:2, implied prayers of repentance in the people's failure to "draw near" to God

Zech. 7:4–5, report of fasting and prayers of mourning

Mal. 3:14, implied prayers of lamentation accompanying mourning rites

## 3. Prayers for others (intercession)

Amos 7:1–9, recorded prayers of intercession

## 4. Prayers for help (petition)

Hosea 2:17, implied prayers for help (and praise?) to the Baals

Hosea 7:14, report of insincere prayer for help as the people "cry out" to their gods, not the LORD

Joel 2:17, recorded prayer of deliverance (as the prophet instructs the priests in what to pray)

Jonah 1:5, report of petition to gods for deliverance

Jonah 1:14, report of petition for pardon

Micah 3:4, implied petition for help unanswered by God

Micah 7:14–17, petition for God to shepherd his people

Zeph. 1:2–6, implied prayers of help to Baal condemned by the prophet (instead of "seeking and inquiring of the LORD")

Zeph. 3:9, implied prayers of help (and praise?) in a coming day when the people will "call on the name of the LORD"

Zech. 1:12, report of prayer of petition by an interpreting angel

Zech. 8:21, report of prayers of help by the nations one day when they "entreat" and "seek the LORD"

Zech. 13:9, report of prayers of help when Israel "calls upon the name of the LORD" in a future day

Mal. 1:9, implied prayers of help (and praise/worship) in the exhortation to "entreat God's favor" (also prayers of invocation/benediction?)

## 5. Prayers of lament (complaint)

Jonah 4:2–3, recorded prayer of lament/complaint

Hab. 1:2–4, recorded prayer of lament/complaint (also prayer of intercession?)

Hab. 1:12–17, recorded prayer of lament/complaint (also prayer of intercession?)

## 6. Prayers for divine justice

Amos 2:6–8; 5:10–12; 8:4–6, sidelight to prayer in link between worship and social justice

Amos 4:1–4, 6–13, sidelight to prayer in the declaration that God is just in regard to the issue of theodicy

Micah 3:9–12; 6:6–8, sidelight to prayer in link between worship and social justice

Zeph. 1:12, implied prayers questioning divine justice

## 7. Prayers of blessing and curse

Mal. 1:14; 2:2 (?); 3:9 (?), reports of prayer in the form of a curse

## 8. Prayers of vow-making and oath-taking

Jonah 1:16, implied prayers of vow-making

Nahum 1:15, implied prayers of vow-making

Zeph. 1:5, implied prayers of oath-taking by the god Molek condemned by the prophet

## 9. Prayers of oracle-seeking

Hosea 4:12, implied prayers (to Baal?) for oracle-seeking

## 10. Prayers of invocation and benediction

Mal 1:9, 14, included in implied prayers of worship/adoration?

# CATALOG OF PRAYER TEXTS IN THE TWELVE PROPHETS BY BOOK

**Hosea**: implied prayers related to false worship, 2:17, 4:12; implied prayer in a summons to repentance and call to worship, 5:15; 10:12; report of insincere prayer, 7:14; recorded prayer (as the prophet instructs the people in a "sinners prayer"), 14:2–3

**Joel**: call to raise a prayer of lament, 1:13; call to fasting and prayer, 2:12–17; recorded prayer of deliverance (as the prophet instructs the priests in what to pray, 2:17)

**Amos**: implied prayer in the call to "seek the LORD," 5:4–5, 6; recorded prayers of intercession, 7:1–9; sidelight to prayer in the link between worship and social justice, 2:6–8; 5:10–12; 8:4–6; sidelight to prayer in the declaration that God is just in regard to the issue of theodicy, 4:1–4, 6–13

**Obadiah**: no prayers in the book

**Jonah**: report of sailors' prayer for deliverance from the storm, 1:5; report of the sailors' prayer seeking pardon from blood guilt, 1:14; implied prayers in the sailors offering of sacrifices and making vows, 1:16; recorded prayer of Jonah's thanksgiving, 2:2–9; report of Nineveh's prayer of repentance 3:8–9; recorded prayer of Jonah's lament, 4:2–3

**Micah**: implied prayer in the threat of God's refusal to hear prayer, 3:4; sidelight to prayer in the link between worship and social justice, 3:9–12; 6:6–8; prophetic liturgy (7:7–20) including a prayer of petition, 7:14–17

**Nahum**: implied prayer in reference to fulfilling of vows, 1:15

**Habakkuk**: recorded prayer of lament, 1:2–4; second recorded prayer of lament, 1:12–17; recorded prayer, a pslamic hymn of thanksgiving, 3:1–19

**Zephaniah**: implied prayers to the false gods Baal and Molek, 1:4–6; implied prayer questioning divine justice, 1:12; implied prayers of repentance in the call to seek the LORD, 2:3; implied prayers of help in the rebuke for not trusting in the LORD or drawing near to God, 3:2; report of prayers (of praise and help?) in the vision of all people calling upon the name of the LORD, 3:9

**Haggai**: no prayers in the book of Haggai, yet the prophet Haggai makes an immense contribution to the prayer life of post-exilic Israel in mobilizing the people to rebuild the Jerusalem temple

**Zechariah**: report of prayer of petition by an interpreting angel, 1:12; report of prayers and fasting, 7:4–5; report of nations one day entreating the LORD, 8:21; report of Israel calling on the name of the LORD in a future day, 13:9

**Malachi**: implied prayer in the exhortation to entreat the favor of God, 1:9; implied prayer in the reference to incense offerings (1:11) and the name of the LORD being reverenced among the nations, 1:14; implied prayers of thanksgiving with the tithe offerings, 3:10; implied prayers of lament accompanying mourning rites, 3:14; report of prayer in the form of a curse, 1:14; 2:2 (?); 3:9 (?)

# TOWARD A THEOLOGY OF PRAYER IN THE TWELVE PROPHETS

An analysis of sample biblical prayer texts from select books of the Twelve Prophets is offered below. The discussion provides the grist for identifying and developing key tenets of a theology of prayer in the Minor Prophets that conclude this study. The use of alternative terms Twelve Prophets and Minor Prophets is intentional. The former may imply an emphasis on the Hebrew Bible and an OT theology of prayer. The latter may imply a biblical theology of prayer that includes reference to the NT as well, since in Christian tradition this is the historical and theological destination of the OT. This review will focus primarily on an Old Testament theology prayer.

# HOSEA

In liturgical contexts, the verb "seek" (Heb. *bqsh*, 5:15; *drsh*, 10:12), may function as a summons to worship or a call to repentance (implying prayer as an element of that religious activity).[15] According to Miller, "the language of 'seeking God' [Heb. *bqš*], while it may on occasion refer to prayers of petition, has in mind the broader reality of a life lived in relationship with the Lord, involving the full devotion of prayer, obedience, and righteousness."[16]

Hosea's final message is a call to repentance (14:1–3), employing the imperative verb "return" (Heb. *shwb*), following standard prophetic convention (cf. 6:1, 7:10, 16). Reminiscent of Joel 2:17, Hosea actually coaches the people in prayer by delineating what they should say to the LORD (14:2b–3). The sample "sinner's prayer" consists of seven lines: three positive statements, three negative ones, and a concluding word of assurance.

> Say to him:
> Forgive all our sins
> and receive us graciously,
> > that we may offer the fruit of our lips.
> Assyria cannot save us;
> > we will not mount warhorses.
> We will never again say, 'Our gods' to what our own hands
> have made,
> > for in you the fatherless find compassion." (NIV)

The emphasis on God's capacities to forgive (Heb. *ns'*), and show compassion (Heb. *rkhm*) echoes the self-proclaimed attributes of the merciful LORD of the Sinai revelation (Exod. 34:6–7). Nogalski summarizes "the image created by this prayer is that of a pious worshiper who offers a vow/sacrifice... [one of] a changed life, a confession to YHWH, and a petition for YHWH to remove the guilt of former actions."[17]

# JOEL

Joel records, presumably, a second charge by the prophet for the people of Zion to gather for a solemn assembly. The prophet's admonition includes a call to repentance (2:12–14) and a summons to communal lamentation (2:15–17). All are ordered to fast and join in prayer led by weeping and contrite priests. In verse 17, the prophet even instructs the priests in what to pray—a prayer of deliverance for the sake of God's reputation, not Israel's:

> Let them say, "Spare your people, O LORD.
>> and do not make your heritage a mockery,
>> a byword among the nations.
> Why should it be said among the peoples,
>> 'Where is their God?'" (NRSV)

Here the prophet instructs the priests both in how to pray and what to pray. We also learn that the LORD took pity on his people and responded to their prayers of lament with the promise of deliverance from the "northern army" and restoration of his covenant blessings for the land and its people—his heritage (2:18–27). Miller notes that Joel's call to repentance and the hope of God's relenting and staying his judgment "are rooted in the same understanding of God's nature that so frustrated Jonah" (cf. Jonah 4:2).[18]

# AMOS

The intercessory prayer of Amos is actually a series of two short prayers in response to three visions of judgment against the northern kingdom of Israel the prophet received from the LORD God (7:1–9). In his first prayer, the prophet petitions God to stay an impending locust plague (7:2). The LORD responds to the prayer of Amos and relents (Heb. *rkhm*), in keeping with his essential character revealed in Exod. 34:6–7, thus the locust plague is averted (7:3). The second prayer is in response to a threatened shower of fire to be sent by God to destroy the land of Jacob (7:4–5). The LORD heard Amos's prayer and relented (7:6). The third vision, plumb line against a wall, forecasts divine judgment against the high places of Israel and the dynasty of Jeroboam II (7:7–9). There is no recorded prayer of response by the prophet to this threat of divine judgment. Miller comments that "the message of unrelenting doom that so characterized his prophecy was rooted in the reality of a situation so bad that eventually Amos could only stand mute before further visions of divine judgment, no longer able to event pray in behalf of the people (Amos 7:7–9; 8:1–3)."[19]

As a sidelight to prayer, Amos calls his audience to "Seek the LORD and live" (Amos 5:4, 5, 6, 14). The theological use of the verb "seek" (Heb. *drsh*) implies repentance and prayer in prophetic calls to return to God and renew covenant relationship with him.[20] Miller elaborates that the use of *drsh* in Amos 5:4–6, 14–15 "is instructive, for there it seems as if the expectancy is that seeking the Lord involves coming to the sanctuary for worship or inquiry, but Amos makes clear that the true seeking of the Lord involves a mode of moral conduct that is absent among the people."[21]

# JONAH

The brief book of Jonah makes several references to prayer, including: a report that sailors "cried out each to his own god" in the midst of a great storm at sea (1:5). Later these same sailors cry out to the LORD seeking divine pardon from bloodguilt over the act of tossing Jonah into the raging sea (1:14). The opening episode of the story concludes with the sailors offering sacrifice and making vows, presumably in the form of prayers, to the LORD (1:16). Next, the prayer of Nineveh's repentance in response to Jonah's proclamation of impending divine judgment is preserved (3:8–9). Finally, the book records two prayers of the prophet Jonah (2:2–9; 4:2–3).

Miller observes that prayers of people crying out to God in trouble and suffering "is one the thematic threads of Scripture."[22] The example of the sailor's prayer in 1:14 is unusual, in that the words of the prayer are cited. The sailors' anguished plea follows the pattern of simple Hebrew prose prayer, consisting of an address, a petition (in this case two related petitions), and a motivation for the petition. It is noteworthy that in this prayer the sailors utter the name of the Hebrew God, YHWH, for the first time. Sasson comments that this verse is the heart of Jonah's first chapter, "for it catches the moment in which illumination finally strikes the sailors…recognizing—as they did not in v 11—that mercy must be obtained not from the sea, but from that very God."[23]

Jonah's psalmic prayer from the belly of the great fish is usually identified as a song of thanksgiving.[24] The prayer poem is framed by prose narratives that set the context of the prayer (1:17 [MT, 2:1]) and the outcome of the prayer (2:10 [MT, 2:11]). Portions of the poem share phraseology with the Psalter (e.g., Jon. 2:2, cf. Pss. 18:6, 118:5, 120:1;

Jon. 2:3, cf. Pss. 42:7; Jon. 2:4, cf. Ps. 31:22).[25] The prayer may be outlined as follows: Jonah's distress, 2:2–3; Jonah's descent into the watery deep, 2:4–6a; Jonah's deliverance, 2:6b–7; Jonah's thanksgiving, vows, and praise, 2:8–9. Stuart claims the prayer psalm captures part of the essence of the book's theological message, "Yahweh is a merciful God."[26] Twice the prophet makes reference to the LORD's holy temple (2:4, 7) alluding to Solomon's prayer of dedication for the temple and its pivotal role in Israel's prayer life (cf. 1 Kings 8).

In tragic and somewhat humorous fashion, Jonah's prayer of thanksgiving in 2:2–9 devolves into a prayer of lament in 4:2–3. Sardonically for Jonah, this is due to the prayer of repentance decreed by the king of Nineveh for animals and people alike in response to the message of divine judgment announced by this Hebrew prophet. Brueggemann comments that "it is this hallmark of divine graciousness that galls Jonah . . . he rebukes YHWH for being who YHWH has always been in the life of Israel…[I]t is clear that Jonah's gratitude voiced in 2:8 has little staying power, for gratitude would have welcomed divine graciousness toward others."[27]

# HABAKKUK

The opening section of the book of Habakkuk (1:2–2:4) is identified as a "pronouncement oracle" by Hawkins, "a type of oracle that seeks to understand how God's will is being worked out in particular human affairs."[28] Balentine describes the unit as an extended dialogue between Habakkuk and God.[29] Regardless, the pericope consists of two prayers of lament (1:2–4; 12–17), each followed by a divine response (1:5–11; 2:2–4). The prophet himself describes his lament as a prayer of a complaint (2:1). Miller elaborates, "Habakkuk's prayers are almost nothing but complaint to God in challenging questions."[30] The prophet concludes his prayers with the bold declaration that he will take up his post like a watchman and wait for God's response (2:1).

Habakkuk's hymnic psalm of thanksgiving is the most extensive prayer text in the Minor Prophets (Hab. 3:1–19). The heading of the composition labels the poem "a prayer" (Heb. tipilleh) of Habakkuk the prophet (3:1). Jonah uses the same expression to describe his cry to God from inside the fish (Jonah 2:7 [MT v. 8]). The term is a general word for prayer often associated with supplications in times of crisis.[31] The prayer is a pastiche of psalmic forms, containing elements of a hymn, a lament, a song of thanksgiving, and a royal psalm. According to Smith, the prayer is best classified as a "liturgy," perhaps used in temple worship during fall festivals as an intercessory prayer.[32] Andersen acknowledges the mix of psalm types in Hab. 3, but settles on the designation of hymn for the prophet's prayer.[33] Broadly, the hymn is defined as a psalm featuring a call to praise or worship God, along with a description of his praiseworthy attributes and or works. Finally, it is beneficial to recognize the epic qualities of Habakkuk's hymnic prayer that draw on the classic themes such as the Exodus from Egypt and the settlement of the land of Canaan.[34]

The prayer proper consists of a theophany (3:3–7), a victory hymn lauding God's triumph over nature and the nations (3:8–15), and the prophet's response to the divine revelation he has received (3:16–19a). While the musical notations in the superscription and subscription of the prayer indicate its probable use in temple worship, it is important to recognize the intimate connection it has with "Habakkuk's particular experience which has dominated the first two chapters of the book."[35] Bruckner finds the main themes of the prayer poem in the refrain of v. 2: standing in awe of the LORD, as depicted in the Teman and Mount Paran theophany (vv. 3–8); recalling his mighty deeds, as rehearsed in God's subduing of initial creation and the nations in Israel's journey from Sinai to Canaan (vv. 9–13a); and prayerful trusting for mercy in the midst of divine wrath (vv. 13b–15), recorded in the prophet's testimony of faithful waiting upon God (vv. 16–19a).[36]

Robertson understands Habakkuk's concluding prayer as a collage, "a collecting of many images to convey an impression both of past experience and of future expectation."[37] The prophet both avows his own hope in this future expectation by his resolve to "wait" for God's answer(s) to his complaints (2:1) and his confession that the righteous will live by their faithfulness (2:4). In a way, Habakkuk's prayer provides a partial answer to his questions about divine justice in the world. Armerding summarizes, "Habakkuk 1–2 appears to emphasize the human agents in the outworking of this pattern; chapter 3 reveals its inward dynamics in the sovereign agency of God, who implements the covenant through whatever earthly means he chooses. Together they form a compelling and tightly meshed testimony to the ways of God in judgment and in grace."[38]

# WHAT HAVE WE LEARNED?

In light of the preceding study, what do the Twelve teach us about prayer?

## The Nature and Practice of Prayer

Not surprisingly, our study of prayer in the Twelve supports other OT prayer texts with regard to matters of time, place, posture, and gesture. Prayer is made without regard to person and takes place at any time, as well as at set times; and in any place, as well as fixed places.[39] What better example of prayer unconditioned by time, place, and persons than the book of Jonah? The narrative records the spontaneous prayers of foreign sailors and a Hebrew prophet, the former at sea in the midst of raging storm, and the latter entombed in a great fish! Yet from the belly of the great fish, Jonah makes reference to God's holy temple, a site of fixed prayer for the Hebrews with implications for cultic prayers at fixed times.

Though there is little direct information in the Twelve, one can assume the typical postures, gestures, and actions of prayers associated with the various forms of prayer were consistent with what is known about such elsewhere in the OT. This would include emotive and bodily motions appropriate to the occasion, whether mourning rites, festivals, solemn assemblies or personal or national crises or good fortune. The Twelve do make references to fasting, weeping, tearing of garments, and the donning of sackcloth with respect to prayers of repentance and mourning (e.g. Joel 2:12; Jonah 3:7–8).

Greenberg notes that "extemporized prayer put no store by a prescribed wording, the basis of its acceptance by God—of God being touched by it—must be the sincerity of the professions made by the pray-er."[40] He further suggests this refined spirituality was rooted "in the popular experience of extemporized prayer, the spontaneous, heartfelt response to God's presence or action."[41] Such was the nature of true prayer for the Twelve prophets, a rending of the heart (Joel 2:12), walking humbly with God (Mic. 6:8), living by faith (Hab. 2:4), esteeming the name of the LORD—the great King (Mal. 1:14; 3:16).

## The Nature of Pray-ers

Miller comments that prayer is most commonly understood "as a plea to God for help."[52] Pray-ers are people in need. This says much about the human condition, our finitude and fallenness, and the world we live in—a "crooked" world according to Qoheleth (Eccl. 1:15).

As pray-ers, people are teachable and prayer is a learned practice. Both Hosea (14:1–3) and Joel (2:17) instruct or "coach" the people (and the priests) in prayers of penitence, as they preach the call to repent and return to the LORD.

Balentine observes that prayer may serve to depict character in the pray-er, or even more subtly function as a means of caricature or parody.[53] Through the prayer hymn of Habakkuk (3:1-19), Habbakuk is portrayed as a devoted follower of YHWH, a man of faith, voicing deep trust in God and filled with awe and praise for the fame of the LORD (Hab. 2:14; 3:2, 16).[54] Habakkuk models courage and staunch conviction about the unrelenting evil and injustice around him as he voices his protests to God for failing to punish rampant sin. The foil of the responses to the problem of evil by prophets like Jonah and Habakkuk is broadly representative of the Hebrew people during the history of the ministry of the Twelve, especially the Assyrian and Babylonian exiles. Balentine well summarizes Habakkuk's prophetic example—the combination of "waiting" and "running" and "what it means for the righteous to 'live'."[55]

## The Nature, Character, and Purposes of God

Even as biblical prayers may offer a depiction of the character of the pray-er, so prayer may also serve "as a means of delineating divine character. Not only what one says to God but also what one says about God provides insight into God's identity."[56] And this is the whole point of theology, "pressing on to know the LORD" (Hos. 6:3). The theological distillations below are representative not comprehensive, offering scaffolding for further theological reflection and development.

The repetition of (imperative) verbs like "seek" and "draw near" in the prayer texts of the Twelve remind us that God is approachable. He desires relationship and communication with his people. God welcomes honesty and transparency in prayer, even to our honest doubt and protest as expressed in prayers of lament and complaint.

The so-called "YHWH creed" (Exod. 34:6–7) is the theological baseline for prayer in the Twelve Prophets (and the OT for that matter). The LORD, the God of the Sinai covenant, is indeed gracious and compassionate—listening and responding to prayer, even to the extent of "relenting" at times of threatened divine judgment (cf. Jonah 3:9).

Habakkuk's sung prayer encapsulates a theology of prayer in the Twelve Prophets, with its emphasis on standing in awe of the LORD, recalling God mighty deeds in the subduing of initial creation and the nations in Israel's journey from Sinai to Canaan, prayerful trusting in divine mercy in the midst of divine wrath, and faithful waiting upon the God despite the present calamity (Hab. 3:1–19).

The theme of repentance is extremely important in the Twelve; it frames the collection which contains numerous calls to and prayers of repentance. We know from another prophet that the LORD, the exalted One, lives with those who are contrite and humble in spirit (Isa. 57:15, 66:2).

We mentioned the work of Hwang and the notion of *missio Dei* in terms of God's dealings with the nations in the Hebrew Prophets. Brueggemann and Hawkins rightly call attention to "internationalism" in the Twelve, including both God's compassion for the nations and his judgment of the nations. Brueggemann comments: "Jonah wants to keep YHWH safely in his own agenda of willful parochialism; but YHWH breaks out of every such formulation."[57] Hawkins recognizes the tension in the books of Jonah and Habakkuk between God's compassion for those outside of Israel and his sovereign rule of the nations as just judge.[58] The Christian church still participates in the *missio Dei* within that very real tension.

The Twelve Prophets ends with a report that the LORD listened and heard the conversation of those who reverenced him (Mal. 3:16). This is why the faithful people of God pray, because God does listen and respond to the prayers of his people. Who knows? The LORD our God may turn and relent and leave behind a blessing—(Joel 2:13–14; Jonah 3:9).

---

1. T. Collins, "The Scroll of the Twelve," in *The Mantle of Elijah*, Biblical Seminar 20 (Sheffield: Academic Press, 1993), 65; David L. Petersen, "A Book of the Twelve?" in *Reading and Hearing the Book of the Twelve*, ed. J. D. Nogalski and M. A. Sweeney, Symposium 15 (Atlanta: Society of Biblical Literature, 2000), 9–10; P. L. Redditt and A. Schart, *Thematic Threads in the Book of the Twelve*, BZAW 325, (Berlin: de Gruyter, 2003); Marvin A. Sweeney, *TANAK: A Theological and Critical Introduction to the Jewish Bible* (Minneapolis: Fortress, 2012), 343.

2. See Mark J. Boda, "Confession as Theological Expression: Ideological Origins of Penitential Prayer," in *Seeking the Favor of God: Volume, I, The Origins of Penitential Prayer in Second Temple Judaism*, ed. M. J. Boda, D. K. Falk, and R. A. Werline; Early Judaism and Its Literature 21 (Atlanta: SBL, 2006), 27, 28.

3. Christopher R. Seitz, "Prayer in the Old Testament" in *Into God's Presence: Prayer in the New Testament*, ed. R. N. Longenecker (Grand Rapids: Eerdmans, 2001), 8.

4. Jerry Hwang, "The *Missio Dei* as an Integrative Motif in the Book of Jeremiah," *BBR* 24:4 (2013): 481. Hwang adopts the definition of *Missio Dei* proposed by Craig Ott, S. J. Strauss, T. C. Tennet, and A. Moreau, *Encountering Theology of Mission: Biblical Foundations, Historical Development, and Contemporary Issues* (Grand Rapids: Baker Academic, 2010), xv, xvii.

5. J. R. Kelly, "Joel, Jonah, and the YHWH Creed: Determining the Trajectory of the Literary Influence," *JBL* 132 (2013): 805–26.

6. Samuel E. Balentine, *Prayer in the Hebrew Bible: The Drama of Divine Human Dialogue*, OBT (Minneapolis: Fortress), 30 (citing E. Staudt, "Prayer and the People in the Deuteronomist" [Ph.D. diss., Vanderbilt University, 1980], 58).

7. Patrick D. Miller, *They Cried to the LORD: The Form and Theology of Biblical Prayer* (Minneapolis: Fortress , 1994), 1.

8. Ibid., 3, 33.

9. See Miller, *They Cried to the LORD*, 33 and H. Peskett, "Prayers in the Old Testament Outside the Psalms" in *Teach Us to Pray: Prayer in the Bible and the World*, ed. D. A. Carson (Exeter, U.K.: Paternoster , 1990), 29–32.

10. So Balentine, *Prayer in the Hebrew Bible*, 31.

11. Herbert Lockyer, *All the Prayers of the Bible* (Grand Rapids: Zondervan, 1959), 156.

12. Balentine, *Prayer in the Hebrew Bible*; Miller, *They Cried to the LORD*; H. Peskett, "Prayers in the Old Testament Outside the Psalms," 29–32.

13. Moshe Greenberg, *Biblical Prose Prayer: As a Window to the Popular Religion of Ancient Israel* (Berkeley: University of California Press, 1983), 44.

14. Seitz, "Prayer in the Old Testament or Hebrew Bible," 17.

15. S. Wagner, "Biqqēsh; Baqqāshāh," *TDOT* 2:237.

16. Miller, *They Cried to the LORD*, 35.

17. James D. Nogalski, *The Book of the Twelve: Hosea-Jonah* (Macon: Smyth & Helwys, 2011), 190.

18. Miller, *They Cried to the LORD*, 278.

19. Ibid., 264.

20. Cf. S. Wagner, "Darash," *TDOT* 3:298–99.

21. Miller, *They Cried to the LORD*, 36.

22. Ibid., 45.

23. Jack M. Sasson, *Jonah*, in AB 24B, ed. David Freedman (New York: Doubleday, 1990), 131.

24. See Douglas Stuart, *Hosea—Jonah*, WBC 31 (Waco: Word Books, 1987), 468.

25. See the discussions of "Illustrative Passages" related to Jonah's canticle in Sasson, *Jonah*, 159–215.

26. Stuart, *Hosea—Jonah*, 473; cf. G. M. Landes, "The Kerygma of the Book of Jonah," *Interpretation* 21 (1967): 3–31.

27. Walter Brueggemann, *Great Prayers of the Old Testament* (Louisville: Westminster John Knox, 2008), 66–67.

28. Ralph K. Hawkins, *While I was Praying: Finding Insights about God in Old Testament Prayers* (Macon, GA.: Smyth & Helwys, 2006), 136.

29. Balentine, *Prayer in the Hebrew Bible*, 183.

30. Miller, *They Cried to the LORD*, 73, 382 (n. 57).

31. Francis I. Andersen, *Habakkuk*, AB 25 (New York: Doubleday, 2001), 268.

32. Ralph Smith, *Micah-Malachi*, WBC 32 (Waco: Word Books, 1984), 114–15.

33. Anderson, *Habakkuk*, 259.

34. See Richard D. Patterson, *Nahum, Habakkuk, Zephaniah* (Chicago: Moody, 1991), 267.

35. Patterson, *Nahum, Habakkuk, Zephaniah*, 226.

36. James Bruckner, *Jonah, Nahum, Habakkuk, Zephaniah*, in NIVAC, ed. Terry Muck (Grand Rapids: Zondervan, 2004), 251.

37. O. P. Robertson, *The Books of Nahum, Habakkuk, and Zephaniah*, NICOT (Grand Rapids: Eerdmans, 1990), 219.

38. C. E. Armerding, "Habakkuk," *EBC* 7: 520, ed. Frank E. Gaebelein.

39. Cf. Michael E. W. Thompson, *I Have Heard Your Prayer: The Old Testament and Prayer* (Peterborough: Epworth, 1996), 215–17.

40. Greenberg, *Biblical Prose Prayer*, 50.

41. Ibid., 51.

42. Miller, *They Cried to the LORD*, 55.

43. Balentine, *Prayer in the Hebrew Bible*, 64.

44. Hawkins, *While I Was Praying*, 136.

45. Balentine, *Prayer in the Hebrew Bible*, 187.

46. Ibid., 187.

47. Brueggemann, *Great Prayers of the Old Testament*, 67.

48. Hawkins, *While I Was Praying*, 131–32, 144–46.

# PRAYER IN THE PSALMS

## TREMPER LONGMAN III

When we think of prayer in the Old Testament, our minds naturally turn to the book of Psalms. After all, the book may be rightly described not only, with Sigmund Mowinckel, as ancient Israel's hymnbook,[1] but also as a book of prayers. The two descriptions are not really different, since the hymns we sing in church today are often sung prayers, and the Psalms, which are also sung, are addressed to God in a prayer-like "I-Thou" form. In Samuel Ballentine's classic study of prayer in the Old Testament, he acknowledges the book as "the most concentrated resource for biblical prayer."[2] Indeed, he decides to treat the Psalms briefly and tangentially in his book since they are so often studied as prayer. In this way, he can concentrate on the neglected prose prayers of the Bible.

While agreeing with Ballentine's observation that the Psalms are a "concentrated resource for biblical prayer," my first observation is that the book is not composed exclusively of prayers, though that is sometimes the impression that is given by students of the book. If "all prayer is directed to God,"[3] then a minority of psalms are prayers pure and simple. In my recent research I determined that only twenty-nine of the one hundred and fifty psalms are composed of direct address to God and thus are prayers in their entirety.[4] These psalms have a purely vertical dimension, addressing God throughout. On the opposite pole, forty-five psalms never speak directly to God, but rather the speaker, perhaps a worship leader, consistently addresses the congregation.[5] The largest group, composing seventy-five psalms, is mixed in their addressee, alternating between speech to God and speech to the congregation.[6] Thus, they can be said to contain prayer, but are not prayers in their entirety. For those keeping count, that leaves only one psalm, Psalm 45, in which the poet addresses neither God nor the congregation, but rather the king on the occasion of his wedding.

Even with this caveat, the book of Psalms is a formidable collection of ancient Israelite prayers. Thus, we will only be able to scratch the surface when we ask the question, "What do we learn about the theology of prayer from the book of Psalms?"

We will answer this question in two stages in keeping with a Christian interpretation of the book. We will first address the question from the perspective of the book in its Old Testament setting, and then we will speak to the subject from the viewpoint of a Christian reading of the book. The latter takes into account the full canonical story and reads the book of Psalms in the light of the coming of Christ.

Let me first of all emphasize the importance of reading the book of Psalms, or any Old Testament book, first from the vantage point of its original human author and audience. We must put ourselves in the place of that original audience, using our readerly imagination to hear the book without recourse to the New Testament. Thus, with Brevard Childs, the Christian reader of the Old Testament must first consider it in the context of its original setting before Christ, what he refers to as the "discrete voice" or "discrete witness" of the passage. Furthermore, as Childs argues, the Christian then reads the text in the light of Christ.[7] After all, Jesus himself said: "'This is what I told you while I was still with you: Everything must be fulfilled that is written about me in the Law of Moses, the Prophets and the Psalms.'[8] Then he opened their minds so they could understand the Scriptures" (Luke 24:44–45).

# COMPOSITION, COLLECTION, AND ORGANIZATION

First, what can we say about the composition, collection, and organization of the book and what implications might this have for a theology of prayer? The answers to these questions are admittedly somewhat speculative and depend in part on one's attitude toward the psalm titles.

There is no doubt that the titles were added by later editors, but virtually every Old Testament book starting with the Pentateuch have inspired additions by later, anonymous editors.[9] There is no record of a book of

Psalms that does not contain the titles found in the Masoretic text.[10] Thus, we should treat these titles as canonical, though our use of the titles still stands if we treat them as non-inspired, though reliable, tradition.[11]

## Composition

Consequently, the titles give us insight into the composition of the psalms. This is specifically true of the authorial and so-called historical titles. The historical titles are titles that name the event in the life of the composer that led to the writing of the psalm in the first place. There are thirteen psalms, all connected to David, that have a historical title (Psalms 3, 7, 18, 34, 51, 52, 54, 56, 57, 59, 60, 63, and 142). The title of Psalm 18 is particularly noteworthy since it explicitly speaks of David's writing activity: "Of David the servant of the Lord. He sang to the Lord the words of this song when the Lord delivered him from the hand of all his enemies and from the hand of Saul. He said."

These historical titles indicate that the psalms were written in response to a concrete historical experience of the composer. For example, Psalm 3's title informs us that it was composed in the aftermath of the time that David, the composer, "fled from his son Absalom." The story of Absalom may be found in 2 Samuel 13:23–17:29, and recounts how David fled Jerusalem at the time of Absalom's rebellion. Though less than one tenth of the psalms have a historical title, I believe that they do give us a window on typical motivations for writing a psalm. They are not written in a vacuum, but rather in response to a concrete historical experience of God's palpable presence or absence in the events of the psalmist's life.

Even so, the prayers that we know of as psalms, while written in response to a concrete historical event, did not embed that event in the psalm itself. Psalm 3 begins:

Lord, how many are my foes!
How many rise up against me!
Many are saying of me,
"God will not deliver him."[12]

It does not begin: Lord, how many are my foes! Even my son Absalom rises against me!

This lack of historical specificity is typical of the psalms, and for a reason. The psalmists, while inspired by concrete events in their lives, wrote their psalms so that others who have similar, though not identical, experiences to their own could use the psalm as a template for their own prayers.

In this, the psalms are similar to modern hymns that were written in response to events in the composers' lives, but were written not to memorialize those events, but rather to provide a model for later worshippers to reflect on their own lives. An example may be seen in the well-known hymn "Amazing Grace." John Newton (1725-1807) wrote the hymn, reflecting on God's mercy shown to him who had been a slave trader before his conversion. When congregations sing "Amazing Grace" today, they rightly do not reflect on the grace that led to Newton's conversion, but on the grace that led to their own.

According to the authorship titles where seventy-four of the one hundred fifty psalms that name him as author, David is the most prolific of composers of the psalms. In 1 Chronicles 16:7, we learn that David, having written a psalm (found in 16:8–36), handed it to Asaph, the chief Levitical musician, demonstrating his awareness that he was writing not just for himself but for the congregation of Israel ("That day David first appointed Asaph and his associates to give praise to the Lord in this manner"). Thus, what we know about the composition of the psalms indicates that they were written with the intent that they would become templates for the prayers of worshippers who come after them.

## Collection and Organization

Having considered the issue of the composition of the psalms, we turn now to the question of the collection and organization of the book. In my opinion, the collection and organization of the psalms is less significant for our primary concern—a theology of prayer. In terms of the former, we know even less about the dynamics of the collection of the psalms than we do about the composition of the individual psalms. Again, if we take the titles, particularly the authorship titles, seriously, the book of Psalms began as early as the time of David, if not Moses, and continues down to the time of the post-exilic period (Pss. 126 and 137).

In terms of the organization of the final form of the book of Psalms, we have to admit that we cannot be certain when the book reached the final form as we know it. Though the final form of the organization of the Psalms cannot be dated, there is no doubt that over time, until that final form was achieved, the organization changed. For one thing, the only editorial note that we get in the book that bears on the subject is no longer the case, though at one point in the transmission of the book of Psalms it must have been. "Thus ends the prayers of David son of Jesse" (72:20). It is impossible to tell whether the different structure of the Psalm scrolls at Qumran is the result of a different order or whether these scrolls are texts that alter the order of the final form for ritual purposes. If the former, then the final form of the book was fixed at a relatively late period before or around the time of Christ.

In any case, debate rages over the significance of the final form of the book as we now have it. Beginning with the publication of Gerald Wilson's groundbreaking Yale dissertation in 1985,[13] different explanations have been offered for the structure of the book and its significance. In brief, Wilson argues that the psalms at the beginning and the end of the five books of the psalms (in particular 2 [since 1 introduces the whole book], 41, 72, and 89, the so-called "seam psalms") provide a narrative coherence to the book since they all contribute to the theme of the rise and fall of the Davidic dynasty. The second two books of the Psalms replace a focus on the Davidic dynasty with a focus on God's kingship, giving the book a messianic impulse.

Elsewhere I critique this particular approach more carefully,[14] but here I would point out that Wilson stretches the interpretation of certain psalms (is Ps. 89 really announcing the demise of the Davidic covenant?), ignores certain seam psalms that do not fit his schema (Pss. 42 and 73, for instance), and also does not recognize psalms, particularly 132, that speaks positively of the Davidic covenant even after its demise. In addition, the mere fact that no one had ever seen this overarching structure of the book before Wilson in 1985 and other attempts to talk about the structure of the book differ from his raises the possibility, indeed the probability, that he has imposed an organizing structure on the book of Psalms rather than discovering one.

Wilson generated a veritable cottage industry of dissertations and publications that have proposed overarching structures to the book of Psalms.[15] The very fact that they are each scholar's vision of the structure is different in and of itself renders the whole enterprise suspicious. If the final editors of the book of Psalms intended a meaningful structure to the book, would not that structure be fairly obvious and not discovered only recently and would not there be agreement at least on the general contours of that structure?

It appears, at least to me, that these attempts have overreached. That is not to deny that there are some generally agreed upon and long-standing comments to be made on the final form of the book. For instance, since the beginning of the history of interpretation, Psalms 1 and 2 have been understood to function as an introduction to the book. Psalm 1 was given initial position to serve as a gatekeeper into the book of Psalms itself understood to be a kind of sanctuary. Just as the sanctuary was a physical holy space where the worshipper could come into the very presence of God, so the book of Psalms was a holy textual space in which the psalmist spoke to God as if he were in his very presence. Just as the physical sanctuary had its gatekeepers who would allow only the righteous to enter, so Psalm 1 speaks of the blessing on the righteous and how the wicked will not stand in "the assembly of the righteous" (v. 5).[16] After entering through the gate (Psalm 1), Psalm 2 then presents a description of the Lord and his anointed. Psalm 3 is thus the first non-introductory psalm. As there is an intentional placement at the beginning of the book, so there is at the end. Psalms 146–150 are characterized by the recurrent refrain Hallelujah. Indeed, Psalm 150 contains one Hallelujah after another, bringing the book to a close with a tremendous doxology.[17] In addition, we should note that as we move from the beginning to the end there is a transition from a predominance of laments to a predominance of hymns. Thus, there is a move from weeping to rejoicing as we move from beginning to end.

Finally, as regards the structure of the book, we should note that it has been divided into five separate books (1–41; 42–72; 73–89; 90–106; 107–150) by the editors who were collecting and organizing the book. We do not know precisely when this division occurred, but we know it was before the close of the Old Testament canon, since Chronicles cites one of the doxologies that concludes the five books (106:48 is cited at 1 Chron. 16:36).[18] Ancient and modern interpreters believe that this fivefold division is an attempt to make a connection to the Torah, also a single book divided into five parts. What would be the significance of this analogy? Simply that this book of prayers to God composed primarily of human words addressed to God are also considered to be God's Word to humans.

# TYPES OF PRAYERS IN THE PSALMS

The next observation is that these psalm-prayers are not all alike in terms of form, emotional expression, or content. Indeed, no two are exactly alike, even Psalms 14 and 53, which are almost identical, have slight, significant differences from each other. Even so, the psalms do, as has been noticed at least since Gunkel, fall into general categories or genres.[19] These genres reflect different modes of prayers. While scholars tend to divide them into different categories, there is a large overlap in how different scholars perceive the different types of psalms. In my own work, I recognize seven types of psalms, three major and four minor.

# THE HYMN, LAMENT, AND THANKSGIVING PSALMS

The three major types of prayers in the book of psalms are the hymn, the lament, and the thanksgiving psalm. The relationship between this triad is captured well by Brueggemann, influenced by Ricouer, as prayers of orientation, disorientation, and reorientation.[20]

The *hymn* is a prayer that expresses unalloyed praise. It is a psalm of orientation, a prayer to God when everything is going well with life. One loves God, other people, and oneself and thus sings a hymn. For example, Psalm 76 is a hymn that celebrates God as a powerful Warrior who wins victories for his people. The psalmist begins by celebrating Zion as the place where God makes his famous name known among his people and where he also prevailed over the weapons of war (vv. 1–3). While these opening verses speak of God in the third person, the psalmist addressed God directly ("you are radiant with light . . ." v. 4) in vv. 4–10. This prayer language celebrates God as the judge who "alone" must "be feared" (v. 7). The psalm ends with the psalmist calling on his hearers to make vows to God (vv. 11–12).

The *lament* is a prayer for people whose lives are broken and troubled; they are psalms of disorientation. The same is true of the five songs of lament within the book of Lamentations.[21] While many hymns address God in the third person, the lament typically appeals to God directly and more consistently in the second person. There are more laments in the book of Psalms than there are hymns, perhaps in recognition that life is typically filled with trouble and chaos. Psalm 120 is a brief lament that begins with the psalmist, the worship leader, announcing his attention to call on God "in my distress" (v. 1). Then, he moves to address God directly and urgently by making an appeal for his help ("Save me, Lord"). Such an invocation and appeal for help is quite typical in a lament and is often followed, as this psalm is, by some kind of general or more specific reference to the danger that the psalmist and/or his community is facing. Here the danger is lying lips and deceitful tongues (v. 2). The end of the psalm indicates that the psalmist is far from Jerusalem and the most palpable symbol of God's powerful presence (the sanctuary). He lives among foreigners who are either at war or plotting to war against the psalmist (vv. 5–7). The psalmist's confidence in God in the midst of trouble is expressed in vv. 3–4, where he addresses the enemy and announces that the enemy's judgment is sure.

No better example of a *thanksgiving* psalm can be found than Psalm 30. A thanksgiving is very similar to a hymn in its positive, joyful mood. The only difference is that the thanksgiving shows awareness of an earlier lament. Thus, it is a psalm of reorientation rather than a psalm of orientation. Psalm 30 begins with the prayer's praise, but his reason suggests a previous problem since God "lifted me out of the depths and did not let my enemies gloat over me" (v. 1). At the heart of the psalm, he remembers how God had made him prosper, but then how he had turned presumptuous and ascribed his well-being to his own power and not God's ("When I felt secure, I said, 'I will never be shaken,'" v. 6). God then abandoned him, and he grew sick. But then he turned back to God, and "you healed me," (v. 2).

# THE WISDOM, REMEMBRANCE, CONFIDENCE, AND KINGSHIP PSALMS

The three major types of prayers (hymns, laments, and thanksgiving) are by far the most frequent, but we should take note of the four minor categories: wisdom, remembrance, confidence, and kingship psalms.

Since these types are less frequently attested, I will treat them more briefly in order to simply introduce them. *Wisdom psalms* share themes, motifs, concerns, forms, and terminology with the wisdom books,

Proverbs, Job, Ecclesiastes, and Song of Songs. Psalm 73 is a prayer that begins by addressing God in the third person, "Surely God is good to Israel, to those who are pure in heart" (v. 1), but then soon addresses God in the second person. Like Job, the psalmist is troubled by the prosperity of the wicked and the suffering of the righteous, among whom he counts himself. However, he comes to a clearer perspective on matters when he "entered the sanctuary of God" (v. 17). Then he realizes that "you (God) place them (the wicked rich) on slippery ground" (v. 18), while "I (the psalmist) am always with you" (v. 23). *Remembrance psalms* are those who look to the past and God's mighty acts to praise the Lord. Some remembrance psalms speak of God in the third person (see Pss. 78 and 136), but Psalm 106 is an example of a remembrance psalm that addresses God in a prayer-like second person. Psalm 106 follows with a remembrance of the people's sinful rebellion against their God who rescues them. The psalm's content fits best with a composition during the time of the exile. The composer likens his generation's rebellion to that of generations past. He puts his hope in the fact that God saved those past generations. Perhaps he will save them as well. While a song of remembrance, the psalm may also be seen as a lament as it calls on God to save them from their present distress. Psalm 23 is a classic and well-beloved example of a *psalm of confidence*. It too opens in the third person ("The Lord is my shepherd," v. 1), but quickly shifts to addressing God directly in a prayer-like fashion ("Even though I walk through the darkest valley, I will fear no evil, for you are with me; your rod and your staff, they comfort me"). Lastly, *kingship psalms* are psalms that are deeply connected to divine and/or human kingship. Psalm 20 in particular is a prayer for the king who is addressed in the second person in vv. 1–5 and then in the third person in vv. 6–9. Interestingly David is named as the author in the title, and it is not impossible that the king could have composed this song, but it is more likely that the song was recited by a third party on behalf of the king. The psalm is a pre-battle song requesting help in warfare, but also expressing confidence in the outcome. Second Chronicles 20:20–21 gives a hint at the pre-battle spiritual preparations and the words of encouragement spoken by the king, as well the role of the priests, and perhaps gives us a glimpse at the type of situation that would have provided a concrete setting for the use of this psalm.[22]

These various types of psalms express every emotion that is known to humanity. Calvin captures this idea in the following quote that I also find illuminating as we consider the Psalm's contribution to a theology of prayer:

> What various and resplendent riches are contained in this treasury, it were difficult to find words to describe... I have been wont to call this book, not inappropriately, an anatomy of all parts of the soul; for there is not an emotion of which anyone can be conscious that is not here represented as in a mirror.[23]

This anatomy of all parts of the soul arises from the brutal honesty of the psalmist, and as a model of prayer invites those who follow and use these prayers to inspire their own prayers to be brutally honest themselves.

# READING THE PSALMS AS CHRISTIANS

Thus, the psalms are the prayers of ancient Israel. They were composed in response to specific events in the life of the composer, but written in a historically non-specific way so that other worshippers can use them as their own prayer. Since, as Calvin states, they present an "anatomy of the soul," there is a prayer for every season of life.[24]

# PRAYING THE PSALMS

We turn now to specific examples to explore how Christians can appropriate the psalms as inspiration for their own prayers. Space will not permit a look at all the genres of the psalms, so we will only consider the three of the most frequent: the lament, the hymn, and a song of confidence.

## Lamenting the Difficulties of Life: Psalm 77

*"I cried out to God for help; I cried out to God to hear me."*

The composer intends for the later user to identify with the first-person speaker. The "I" in this case is not the composer but the struggling worshipper. As the first person speaker goes on, he does not specifically identify the issue that led to such distress, and so the later person who prays this psalm can fill in the particulars of his or her own life.

The first person speaker, now the contemporary pray-er, goes on to complain to God about how God has forgotten and abandoned him or her. In a series of rhetorical questions (vv. 7–8), the pray-er challenges God and implicitly accuses him of harm. In this way, the psalm as a model of prayer encourages us today to be bold and honest in our prayers to God.

As is typical in laments, this prayer turns from anguish to joy and confidence (vv. 10–13). What is not typical about this particular example is that the psalmist expresses reasons for the change of mood. The psalmist gains confidence to live in a trouble present and hope for an uncertain future by turning to the past, namely God's mighty acts of deliverance and in particular the crossing of the Sea at the time of the Exodus. The latter inspires confidence and trust because it demonstrates that God is able to rescue those who are beyond human help.

The Christian who prays Psalm 77 can also think of the Exodus and remember that our God is a God who saves. But, of course, we know that Jesus was the fulfillment of the Exodus.[25] The prophets anticipated a second and ultimate exodus (Isa. 40:1–5; Hos. 2:14–20) and the Gospels point to Jesus as the fulfillment (Mark 1:1–3). He is the one who crossed the Sea (through his baptism, see 1 Cor. 10:1–6), withstood the forty days of temptations in the wilderness (Matt. 4:1–11), delivered the law from the mountain (Matt. 5–7), and died on the eve of the annual commemoration of the deliverance from Egypt. He is our Passover lamb (1 Cor. 5:7). Thus, we can look back to the cross to gain confidence for the present and hope for the future.[26]

## Praising Jesus: Psalm 104

Psalm 104 alternates between a prayer-like appeal to God in the second person ("Praise the Lord, my soul. Lord my God, you are very great; you are clothed in splendor and majesty," v. 1) and speaking of God in the third person ("The Lord wraps himself in light as with a garment . . ." v. 2a). Perhaps this alternation can be explained by the fact that the prayer leader both addresses God and the congregation. Psalm 104 is a hymn that celebrates God as creator and sustainer of all life on earth. The psalmist praises God by describing poetically his creation: "How many are your works, Lord! In wisdom you made them all; the earth is full of your creatures" (v. 24). This powerful hymn concludes by the pray-er's commitment to praise God "all my life" (v. 34).

The Christian who prays Psalm 104 thinks of Jesus who participated in the creation process. The opening of the Gospel of John speaks of Jesus as the Word who was with God and "through him all things were made; without him nothing was made that has been made. In him was life, and that life was the light of all mankind. The light shines in the darkness, and the darkness has not overcome it" (1:3–5). The one who said, "I am the light of the world. Whoever follows me will never walk in darkness, but will have the light of life" (John 8:12) also spoke of appearing on a cloud at the end of time, rescuing his people and bringing judgment on those who resist him (Matt. 24:30; Mark 13: 26; 14:62; Luke 21:27; Rev. 1:7).[27] The author of Hebrews cites 104:4 to support his argument that Jesus is superior to the angels (Heb. 1:7).

## Confidence in the Midst of Turmoil: Psalm 11

Psalm 11 speaks of God in the third person rather than the second, but still is the template of a prayer for us today as we identify with the psalmist who speaks in the first person as he expresses his trust in God in the midst of trouble. When life goes wrong, our first impulse is to utter laments to God. If God answers our lament, we then start singing thanksgiving songs, but if he chooses not to respond to our cries for help, we then should begin to pray psalms of confidence to him, knowing that in spite of the ongoing trouble, he is still with us.

In Psalm 11, the psalmist, with whom we identify, castigates the attempts of those who want us to flee our troubles as if God is not there to take care of us. He does not need to flee because God is his refuge even in the light of the assault of his enemies.

In the face of the wicked that seek to destroy us to our very foundations (v. 3), we can remain calm in the light of the fact that God is with us (v. 4). He cares for the righteous and will bring justice against the wicked.

The Christian who prays this psalm has even more reason than the psalmist to express this kind of confidence. After all, in the Old Testament time period, God made his presence known in the sanctuary in the symbolism of the Ark of the Covenant which was thought to be the footstool of God's throne.

Christians live in the period when "the Word became flesh and made his dwelling among us" (John 1:14). When Jesus departed to sit at the right hand of the Father, he promised to send the Holy Spirit to be with us. God indeed makes his presence known to his people today in a more palpable manner than during the Old Testament period. Thus, we have even more reason to sing the songs of confidence than those who wrote them in the period before the coming of Jesus.

# CONCLUSION

The book of Psalms is often called the hymnbook of the Old Testament. In this chapter we wanted to draw attention to the book as a book of prayers. It was written in response to specific historical events in the life of the composer, but the composer does not embed the concrete events that inspired his writing, but wrote in such a way that later worshipers, even Christians today, can use these texts as models of our own prayers.

---

1. Though he did not think it was "collected just for this purpose," he did believe that it likely became "the hymnbook of the Second Temple" and that many psalms were used in the worship of the second temple. See Sigmund Mowinckel, *The Psalms in Israel's Worship* (Nashville: Abingdon Press, 1962), 2.

2. Samuel Balentine, *Prayer in the Hebrew Bible: The Drama of Divine-Human Dialogue*, in OBT (Minneapolis: Fortress, 1993), 16.

3. Balentine, *Prayer*, 33.

4. Pss. 5, 8, 15, 17, 38, 39, 51, 61, 65, 70, 71, 72, 73, 74, 75, 79, 80, 83, 86, 88, 90, 92, 93, 94, 119, 139, 141, 142, 143.

5. Pss. 1, 2, 11, 14, 24, 29, 33, 34, 37, 46, 47, 49, 50, 53, 63, 78, 81, 87, 91, 95, 96, 98, 100, 103, 105, 107, 110, 111, 112, 113, 114, 117, 121, 122, 127, 128, 129, 133, 134, 136, 146, 147, 148, 149, 150.

6. Pss. 3, 4, 6, 7, 9, 10, 12, 13, 16, 18, 19, 20, 21, 22, 23, 25, 26, 27, 28, 30, 31, 32, 35, 36, 40, 41, 42, 43, 44, 48, 52, 54, 55, 56, 57, 58, 59, 60, 63, 64, 66, 67, 68, 69, 76, 77, 82, 84, 85, 89, 97, 99, 101, 102, 104, 106, 108, 109, 115, 116, 118, 120, 123, 125, 126, 130, 131, 132, 135, 137, 138, 140, 142, 144, 145.

7. Brevard S. Childs, *Biblical Theology of the Old and New Testaments: Theological Reflection on the Christian Bible* (Minneapolis: Fortress, 1993), 76.

8. The Psalms here refers to the Ketubim, the entire third part of the Hebrew canon, but certainly includes the book that Christians refer to as Psalms and Jews as Tehillim.

9. In terms of the Torah, the so-called post- and amosaica at a minimum. See Tremper Longman III, *How to Read Genesis* (Downers Grove: InterVarsity, 2005), 45–6.

10. The Septuagint and the Peshitta have these titles and more.

11. For an alternative view, see Brevard Childs, "Psalm Titles and Midrashic Exegesis," *JSS* 16 (1971): 137–50; E. Slomovik, "Toward an Understanding of the Formation of Historical Titles in the Book of Psalms," *ZAW* 91, (1979): 350–81.

12. Unless otherwise indicated, all translations are taken from the NIV.

13. Gerald H. Wilson, *The Editing of the Hebrew Psalter* (Chico: Scholars Press, 1985).

14. Most recently, Tremper Longman III, *Psalms*, TOTC, (Downers Grove: InterVarsity, 2014), 33–6.

15. Erich Zenger (editor), *The Composition of the Book of Psalm*, BETL 238, (Leuven: Uitgeverij Peeters, 2010) contains dozens of articles with references to even earlier literature on the subject of the editing of the psalms.

16. That the Psalms are a literary sanctuary is not a new insight since Jerome described it as a "large house" (*magna domus*) with Psalms 1 and 2 serving as an entrance to this house. More recently Janowski rightly said that "the Psalms…are something like a *templum spirituale*, a temple not of stones but of words with the proem of Ps. 1–2 as wide "entrance portal" and the final Hallel of Ps. 146–150 as a resounding 'keystone'" (B. Janowski, *Arguing with God: A Theological Anthropology of the Psalms* [Louisville: Westminster John Knox, 2013], 348).

17. Tremper Longman III, "From Weeping to Rejoicing: Psalm 150 as the Conclusion to the Psalter," in *The Psalms: Language for All Seasons of the Soul*, ed. D. Howard and A. Schmutzer (Chicago: Moody, 2013): 219–28.

18. Hans-Joachim Kraus, *Psalms 60-150*, CC (Minneapolis: Fortress, 1993), 322.

19. Hermann Gunkel, *Die Psalmen*, 6th edition (Gottingen: Vanderhoeck and Ruprecht, 1986); Hermann Gunkel and Joachim Begrich, *Introduction to the Psalms: The Genres of Religious Lyric of Israel* (Macon: Mercer University Press, 1985).

20. Walter Brueggemann, *The Psalms and the Life of Faith*, ed. Patrick D. Miller (Minneapolis: Augsburg Fortress, 1995), 3–32.

21. For discussion of the genre of lament in the book of Lamentations, see, e.g.: F. W. Dobbs-Allsopp, *Weep O Daughter of Zion: A Study of the City-Lament Genre in the Hebrew Bible* (Rome: Pontifical Biblical Institute, 1993); Paul W. Ferris, Jr. *The Genre of the Communal Lament in the Bible and the Ancient Near East* (Atlanta: Scholars Press, 1992); Tod Linafelt, *Surviving Lamentations: Catastrophe, Lament, and Protest in the Afterlife of a Biblical Book* (Chicago: University of Chicago Press, 2000). For an interpretation of Lamentations, see my *Jeremiah, Lamentations*, UBCS (Baker, 2008).

22. Gerald H. Wilson, *Psalms 1-75*, NIVAC (Grand Rapids: Zondervan, 2002), 381–82.

23. Quoted in Herbert Lockyer, "In Wonder of the Psalms," *Christianity Today* 28, (March 2, 1984): 76.

24. David Hubbard, *Psalms for All Seasons* (Grand Rapids: Eerdmans, 1973).

25. Fully developed in Tremper Longman III, *How to Read Exodus* (Downers Grove: InterVarsity Press, 2009), 145–55.

26. For further studies on the Christian appropriation of lament, see Dan B. Allender and Tremper Longman, *Cry of the Soul: How Our Emotions Reveal Our Deepest Questions about God* (Colorado Springs: NavPress, 1994); David J. Cohen, *Why O Lord?: Praying Our Sorrows* (Milton Keynes, UK: Paternoster, 2013); Glenn Pemberton, *Hurting with God: Learning to Lament with the Psalms* (Abilene: ACU Press, 2012).

27. The immediate antecedent is Daniel 7:13–14.

# PRAYER IN THE WISDOM LITERATURE

ELAINE A. PHILLIPS

## INTRODUCTION: CONFESSION, PETITION, ACCUSATION, AND INTERCESSION IN WISDOM LITERATURE

Knitting together the references and allusions to prayer in the biblical wisdom literature is a challenge, notably because the texts themselves are so disparate. No doubt thinking of Proverbs, James Crenshaw claimed that Wisdom Literature is characterized by the "conviction that men and women possess the means of securing their well-being—that they do not need and cannot expect divine assistance."[1] On the other hand, we catch fleeting glimpses of the outpouring of Job's appeals to God in his alternating petitions and accusations.

Prayer, lodged deeply in the brokenness of human experience, calls for help and healing and trusts that God will respond. As we probe further, however, we must inquire if that description is too narrow. Are not praise and blessing also prayer? What about cursing? In fact, imprecations often come out of the same anguished circumstances that prompt prayer. Perhaps we should include all attempts at "conversation" with God.[2] It appears our initial task is to investigate both the "vocabulary" and purposes of prayer.

The limitations of a solely lexical study are immediately evident. When we start by looking for *tefillah* and related cognates, we find in the Wisdom texts a rather slim sample. Additional key Hebrew terms include *darash* (seek, inquire), *'atar* (entreat), *yadah* (thank), *barakh* (bless). With minor exceptions, however, very few of these have a high profile in the Wisdom Literature. "Calling upon the Name of the Lord" and "X said to God…" are signals in narrative portions of Scripture but are also sparsely represented here.[3] Clearly, we need to readjust our focus and pay particular attention to perceived intentions of the biblical writers and speakers as the themes of confession, petition, accusation, and intercession surface.

Paradoxically, God's oft-felt absence, along with dark anger, agonizing questions, and protest, drive us to prayer.[4] Job leaps to mind. In fact, much of what Job says might be characterized as his journey *toward* prayer. Thus we face a further question: Is there a distinct boundary marker on the road between self-focused lament and fledgling attempts to call on an apparently silent God? Perhaps not.

Strictly speaking, prayer is the way we engage God in the chaos of our lives when expectations have been shredded by agonizing experience.[5] That engagement means dialogue. The individual who has turned to God seeks God's attention and response because the petitioner *knows* that prayers are heard in heaven; prayer is at the intersection between heaven and earth.[6] Even when God's responses are perceived as unsatisfactory, the truly praying individual doggedly continues and is remarkably satisfied in the end.[7] Nevertheless, getting to the point of dialogue may involve a myriad of partially formulated expressions, some more felicitous and directed than others. How do we characterize the internal rumblings of the petitioner when that intersection between heaven and earth appears initially to be blocked? We would be remiss if we did not explore the winding pathway toward the actual dialogue.

# A "PRAYER LENS" ON WISDOM LITERATURE TEXTS—OVERVIEW OF INTERPRETIVE ISSUES

It is no secret that the three biblical wisdom texts are head-scratchingly different from each other. That has baffled students of Wisdom in the past and is the issue that affects this theological exploration more than any other of the academic discussions of these texts.

## Proverbs

The book of Proverbs primarily has to do with character as it is manifest in interpersonal words, appeals, and actions. Because Proverbs is a book of practical instruction, the character- consequences nexus is at the heart of this compilation of sayings. While the first chapters are shot through with Wisdom's appeal to humankind, the glimpses of communication in the other direction (from humans to God) are rare and fleeting. Furthermore, the observational nature of many of the sayings seems removed from the emotion-wracked circumstances that prompt prayer. Thus there is little in the book that explicitly enjoins prayer.[8] Nevertheless, the observations often address deeply emotional issues that call forth prayer.

In addition, there are significant connections between covenant and the biblical proverbs, not least of which is the fear of the Lord. Covenant expectations involve responses of obedience and awareness of consequences for both righteousness and otherwise. When prayer is mentioned, it is in conjunction with the "prayer of the righteous." We will address this further.

While it is outside the parameters of this chapter to address the knotty issues of composition, authorship(s), and the date of Proverbs, the connection of Solomon's name with sections of the book (1:1; 10:1; 25:1) is significant. His prayer, blessing, and festival celebration at the Temple dedication (1 Kings 8:22–9:9; 2 Chron. 6:1–7:22) draw together covenant obedience, prayer, and sacrifice in the context of that sacred space. These aspects of Israel's cult make their appearance in Proverbs 15:8, to be discussed below.

## Ecclesiastes (Qoheleth)

Lest we too quickly dismiss Ecclesiastes (Qoheleth), at least one scholar has styled it a series of "confessions" in its entirety.[9] While that contention might be extreme, nevertheless the central interpretive question, the meaning of *hevel*, is important because it shapes how we read these ruminations from Qoheleth. Does *hevel* bear within it the depressing tones of futility and "meaninglessness"? Or should our interpretation be shaped by the basic meaning of *hevel*—"breath" or "vapor"? The nature of the book is profoundly affected by whether we see Qoheleth as a pessimistic cynic (who, by the very nature of his cynicism, could not and would not bring himself to pray) or as someone overwhelmed at the brevity of life and finality of death. In the latter case, this agonizing lament, culminating in an explicit affirmation of the fear of the Lord, is shaped by perception of *need*, notably the need to come to grips with the worst enemy, death. That backdrop is not unimportant in our quest.

## Job

Job might be considered a series of long, quite unorthodox outbursts and prayers sandwiched between the narrative chapters and interrupted periodically by the friends' misguided pontifications. A host of interpretive issues arises in conjunction with this towering figure. I will simply mention two that are germane to our pursuit of the theology of prayer.

First, the relationship between the prose introduction and epilogue, and the poetic dialogues is a key issue. What the reader learns about Job's character in the introduction and what God says to Eliphaz about Job in the epilogue raise complex interpretive questions regarding Job's words in the intervening dialogues. How can the pious Job of the prose narrative be the same anguished and angry Job who unleashes torrents of accusations against God? Even if the prose and poetic materials were two disparate texts later brought together, at some point this apparent dissonance needs to be addressed, especially since there are profound implications regarding prayer. A second and related matter is the nature of God's responses. They appear ill-suited to the deep concerns of Job expressed throughout both the dialogues and his subsequent monologue. How is this in any way expressive of the covenant relationship that we expect to find in prayer?

# WHAT THE TEXTS SAY—AND MEAN

At this point, the task is to present specific texts and themes, all the time recognizing that much is occurring at deeper levels.

## Proverbs

The Hebrew word for "prayer" (*tefillah*) is used only three times in Proverbs. That does not mean, however, that our sojourn in Proverbs will be brief; there will be additional allusions.

15:8—**Sacrifice** of the **wicked** (is) an **abomination** to the LORD, but **prayer** of the **upright** (*yesharim*) (is) His pleasure.[10]

15:29—The LORD is **far from** the **wicked** but **prayer** of the **righteous** (*tsaddiqim*) He will **hear**.

28:9—The one who turns his ear from hearing the *torah*, even his **prayers** are an **abomination**.

Several initial observations are in order. Wickedness is antithetical to effective prayer. The two are impossible bed-fellows because prayer is covenantal communion with God, whereas all activities of the wicked shatter that relationship. Second, "sacrifice" is used in a parallel construction with "prayer" in 15:8. The wicked person attempts both sacrifice and prayer (28:9), but both are the epitome of presumptuous hypocrisy—an "abomination" and "detestable" (in both cases, the word is *to'evah*) to the covenant LORD. By contrast, as the righteous person prays, the Lord is pleased (15:8) and hears (15:29). Hearing goes both ways—or not; God hears the prayers of the righteous even as the wicked are busy "turning a deaf ear" to the law, God's word to humans.

Expanding beyond specific terminology for prayer, we find that the one who spurns the appeal of Wisdom and then calls out to Wisdom will experience the horror of silence in response—and then mockery (1:22–32). Again, hearing is intended to go both ways. Effective covenant communication depends on obedience. From another perspective, the hardened reprobate ruins his own life and yet his heart rages against the Lord (19:3), not exactly prayer as we think of it, but some form of communication!

Then there is the honest prayer of chapter 30:7–9—"Two things I have asked from you; do not refuse me before I die. Emptiness and lying words keep far from me; poverty and wealth don't give to me. Let me tear my allotted bread, lest I am sated and deceive and say, 'Who is the LORD?' Or lest I am made poor and steal, and defame the name of my God." The first part of the request needs no elaboration. The malignancy of deception is all too obvious and insidious; the author knows he needs help warding it off and prays for that help. Lying is a high profile abomination to the Lord throughout the book of Proverbs. The second petition, however, elicits an explanation in the text. After all, there is a certain amount of ambiguity about poverty and wealth in Proverbs, so here the petitioner launches into his reasoning. It makes sense to desire escape from poverty—fearing the temptation to provide by illicit means and the shame of bringing the Lord's name down—but riches? Nevertheless, the primary pitfall of riches could not be clearer—that beguiling appeal of self-sufficiency and its accompanying pride. Just as devastating as dishonoring God by theft is dishonoring the Master of the Universe by rejecting and ignoring Him. Thus, there is a need for fervent prayer.

Proverbs 16:3 implies prayer as the avenue for committing human plans into God's care all the while emphasizing that God is the one who arranges and directs.[11] Accompanying that is trust. "Trust in the Lord with all your heart . . . In all your ways acknowledge Him and He will make straight your paths" (3:5–6) presumes an attitude of prayer. The same is true of the righteous person who knows that "the Name of the Lord is a strong tower" and runs to it for safety (18:10). Likewise, the one who fears the LORD "rests fully, not being touched by evil" (19:23). In fact, the fear of the Lord is the grounds for all appeals to the Lord, a matter we will revisit in regard to Job.

One of the worst kinds of trouble—wholesale injustice—prompts the admonition not to take revenge but *wait* for the LORD who will deliver (20:22). The fact that God is acknowledged as Defender and the One who takes up the case of the poor suggests that they are indeed crying out to God at injustices (22:22–23, 23:10–11). And while there is some question as to whether God is the object of the outcry in 21:13, the sobering measure-for-measure response is clear: the one who shuts his ear to the cry of the poor will cry out but not be answered. The matter of obedience to the covenant is eminently evident here; Deuteronomy warns that the poor who are abused in the workplace or in the matter of overwhelming debt may cry out to the Lord and God will hear that prayer and act accordingly (Deut. 15:9, 24:15).

## Ecclesiastes

Ecclesiastes presents a conundrum. While Crenshaw claimed that Ecclesiastes is devoid of any semblance of prayer,[12] Brown suggested that *all* of Ecclesiastes is confessional.[13] Avoiding these "extremes" (with a nod to Eccl. 7:18c), however, we want to address the admonition about vows (5:1–7). Qoheleth warns against offering "the sacrifice of fools," and that is followed directly by the warning not to be hasty with words, not to utter anything in our hearts before God, not to multiply words, and make absolutely certain to keep vows. This juxtaposition implies that the sacrifice of fools is a sacrifice awash in empty verbiage that was intended to sound like a well-spoken vow. Is a vow a prayer? It seems so. In fact, vows are particularly powerful petitions because they attempt to harness God's response to the faithful expectations of the person making the vow. And what is the harness? It is a promise of sacrifice of some kind. Qoheleth simply says: Be careful here! Words had better be followed by actions.

In contrast to Proverbs, Ecclesiastes makes no mention of human outcry, even though injustice and oppression are evident. Nor are people noted as gratefully acknowledging God's good gifts of wealth, possessions, relationships, honor, and work. In fact, the avenue between heaven and earth is not explicitly traversed apart from the warning about vows.

## Job

Job's communications to God, unacknowledged for a painfully long time, are woven into the complex fabric of the poetic dialogues. Ironically, just as his human dialogue partners failed him miserably, so also God failed Job as a "dialogue" partner until the very end. Nevertheless, Job continued to pursue that relationship even though his unorthodox utterances, moving back and forth between painful rumination about God and address to God, caused his friends near apoplectic fits. From the depths of his despair and pain, Job ventured into the hiddenness of God to demand the latter's response.

Prior to these direct addresses, however, we do have the brief but highly significant indication that Job regularly interceded on behalf of his children (1:5). We also learn that Job feared the Lord and shunned evil (1:1, 8; 2:3), two characteristics that would make his prayer effective according to the Proverbs metric. In the midst of his anguish, he alluded to this previous practice of prayer and knowledge of God's responses (12:4b), and his deep sense of God's "friendship" in better days (29:2–5)."[15]

In the meantime, Job lamented every facet of his ruptured being. Chapter 3 is foundational to understanding the depth of Job's torment and the horror that drove him first to imprecation, and only later to prayer. After the seven days of silent presence of his friends, Job unveiled his tormented existence and interminable suffering. Night, darkness, cloud, and deep shadow, the realm that was aligned against God, are the forces that Job implored to overwhelm the light and the day of his birth. In the second part of chapter 3, Job expressed indirectly his overwhelming desire for death; he later refocused it as an explicit plea to God (cf. chapters 7 and 10). In a nutshell, Job cursed days and longed for death and that latter emphasis became a steady drumbeat!

In response to Eliphaz's attempt to console and cajole, Job said: "Oh, that my request might come, that God would grant my hope, that God would be willing to crush me, that he would loose his hand and violently cut me off! Then I would yet have my consolation and I would respond even in unrelenting anguish—that I had not denied the words of the Holy One" (6:8–10).[16] Job preferred death to betrayal of trust in God—remarkable in any circumstance. And he pleaded for it. Job further accused God of unpleasant visitations (7:13–14), so terrifying that Job would rather have God leave him alone. "My whole being (*nephesh*) would choose strangling; death, rather than my bones. I despise. I would not live forever. Cease from me; because my days are a breath (*hevel*)" (7:15–16). Job asked God if he enjoyed oppressing and rejecting Job (10:3). In tones of perplexed outrage, he directly questioned God: Why did you shape me so carefully, just to destroy that product of your creativity (10:8–12)? In fact, Job "both complains because God is too near and also grieves over the fact that the deity has withdrawn into the heavens."[17]

The drumbeat continued: Job's testimony to God's gift of life (10:12) gave way to his wish that he had not lived following his birth (10:18) and a plea that God turn away from him so that he might have a fleeting moment of joy before the utter darkness of death (10:21–22). With poignant longing, Job intimated that when God *would* care enough to search for him, it would be too late (7:21). Nevertheless, he also expected that God would lovingly call, and Job would answer (14:15). These were not all distant third person ruminations; some he directly addressed to God. At the same time, Job did not employ the traditional language of prayer, where brokenness is expected to elicit God's compassion. His experience told him otherwise. He charged God with a divine scrutiny that made him the object of God's violence.[18]

In fact, Job pressed for an audience with God (13:22) as part of his second explicit challenge: "Only do not do two things to me; then from you I will not be hidden: Distance your hand far from me, and do not torment me with your terrors. Summon and I will answer, or I will speak and you will respond to me" (13:20–22). Job wanted the dialogue reinstated! Job went on to accuse God of *hidden* hostility, asking the reasons for his predicament, and returning to the very real possibility of his own sin (13:23–26). He had already agonized over it, accusing God of being determined to find him guilty (9:28–31; 10:13–15), writing down his offenses, and shackling him (13:26–27). Job begged for forgiveness in place of the torment, using the term *hatathi* ("I have sinned"), and expecting pardon and forgiveness (7:20–21).

In this first cycle of dialogue (chap. 4–14), Job steadily moved toward directly addressing God, interspersing those pleas with words addressed to his human audience. Choon-Leong Seow labeled 13:20–22 "theological refraction," suggesting that Job was telling his friends what he *would* say to God but could not because of the perceived disparity between God and himself. Thus it was only "imagined conversation."[19]

The tone changed in the second round. Job lashed at God with brutal honesty—"surely now I am exhausted; you have devastated my entire company" (16:7). *God* was his adversary and had assailed him, torn him, shattered and crushed him, cast him into the clutches of wicked people, and had attacked him repeatedly (16:7–14). This was the divine Warrior who, in other biblical contexts, came to fight for His beleaguered people. Here that Warrior was cudgeling a broken individual.[20] What is astonishing is that this broken person continued to address God—"as my eyes pour out tears to God" (16:20b) even as he cast his sea of words about pain, despair, injustice, dishonor, and horror at the hand of God against the rocky shores of judgmental listeners. "Have pity on me," Job cried, "Have pity on me; you are my friends! For the hand of God has struck me" (19:21). There did come a point where Job ceased to plead with God—almost as if he had given up on that project. Prayer gave way to talking about God instead (chap. 19, 21, 23–24, 26–27) until his final accusation. Then, in no uncertain terms, Job nailed God: "I cry out to you, but you do not answer me; I have stood up, but you merely consider me. You turn cruelly against me; with the might of your hand you attack me" (30:20–21). Following that, Job uttered an extended oath, not directed *to* God but designed to compel God to respond. In the absence of the dialogue of prayer, Job forced the issue this way.

But, here is another angle. In the midst of his strongest declarations about God's responsibility for his plight (9:30–31; 16:7–14), Job longed for a mediator, advocate, and intercessor (9:33–34; 16:19–21). Job knew that office well; his had been a life of prayer for others. Sadly, no others around him were taking on the role. Because there was no recourse to any human arbitrator, Job knew that his witness must be found in heaven (16:18–21). That meant that God was both Defender and Adversary; Job addressed God with both of those identities firmly established, interweaving accusations and petitions.

It is clear that Job and his friends had radically different ideas about the purposes of prayer. The friends were intent on prayer as a vehicle, perhaps a rather ossified one, for confession and praise. At the same time, their words were not simply pious platitudes. They enjoined Job to prayer, affirming its power to lead beyond his torment. The spiritual trajectory of prayer is from the present to a hopeful future.[21] Thus, they urged Job to penitential prayer, expressing confidence that God would respond.[22] Eliphaz counseled Job to appeal to God, admonishing him to sing a doxology as a confession of guilt (5:8–26).[23] Bildad and Zophar likewise enjoined Job to plead with the Almighty and stretch out his hands to God, putting away his sin (8:5; 11:13–14). In other words, "repent and confess"! In the second cycle of the dialogue, Eliphaz reprimanded Job for diminishing prayer before God (15:4b). The word translated "prayer" (sikhah) represents "visible and audible manifestation of piety (compare Ps. 119:97, 99)."[24] Thus, Eliphaz understood Job's words as prayer even though he did not think they passed muster. In fact, he was dismayed at the raw outbursts of Job's prayers (15:12–13).

Elihu merits a brief mention as his contribution significantly turned around the friends' approach. They had been pressing Job to engage in prayerful confession in order to be renewed. Instead, Elihu's theological formulation involved the provision of a ransom just at the seemingly hopeless point of death; that would elicit a confession of wonder at the redemptive grace and favor that was unmerited (33:26–28). In other words, Elihu endorsed the prayer language but also knit it together with Job's legal metaphor.[25]

Job defied the practice of prayer advocated by the friends as he lamented and attacked God head-on. His legal approach employed an entirely different metaphor from that of prayer. Instead of appealing to a benefactor for mercy and hope of restoration, his hermeneutical model pursued the truth:[26] Challenge, interrogation, accusation—and trust. Why, he asked, was God doing this to him? Why, we ask, did Job continue to cling to his memory of the relationship and *pray* to his hidden God?[27]

God's means of answering Job's prayers—the whole array of them—were decidedly off the charts in every possible way. Job's accusations and challenges and his oath both drew God out of his silence and submerged any further words from Job.

In light of the overwhelming presence of God and God's radical refocusing on his sovereign wisdom embedded in creation, how are we to understand Job's final words in 42:1–6? This "confession" is notably fraught with translation/interpretation challenges. What sounds on the surface like contrition about his over-reaching demands for vindication and sinful accusations could also be Job's turning away from his humiliating posture and declaring his disdain for God.[28] Following directly on Job's affirmation that his ears had heard of God "and now, my eye has seen you" (v. 5), verse 6 is the focal point of the conundrum: "Therefore, I reject (or "despise"—*ma'as*) and repent (*nikham*) concerning (*'al*) dust and ashes." It is not clear what Job "rejected" or "despised." The verb is never used reflexively, so it is unlikely that he "despised himself" as the NIV renders it. Did he despise God to whom he had just referred? Or was he retracting the case, complete with the set of oaths that he made? Do these two verbs together indicate that Job gave up his role as indomitable defendant? Whatever the tentative conclusions in this regard, Job had stood his ground and this is a prayer—of sorts.[29]

What is of even greater interest, however, in stitching together the whole theological fabric of the book, is what God said in the epilogue. In light of what each of the participants had contributed in the course of the soliloquies and dialogues, God's rebuke in 42:7–8 is possibly the crux of the interpretation of Job and, in fact, it zeroes in on the matter of prayer.[30]

Twice the Lord told Eliphaz that He was angry with the friends "because you have not spoken unto (*'el*) Me in the right manner (or "truth," *nekhonah*) as my servant Job has" (42:7–8). While modern translations[31] render this dual testimony about Job's friends and Job as a matter of speaking the truth *about* God, the Hebrew is simply *'el* which, in its most general usage, indicates motion or direction towards, either physical or mental.[32] This is especially true with a verb meaning "to speak." To be sure, a preposition that is so extensively used as this one has a wide range of nuanced meanings and "with regard to" can be one of them. It is not the best rendition here, however, and that case is strengthened by consulting the earliest translations of this text. Both the Septuagint and the Targum on Job have simply "to" or "unto" as the meaning. What this means is that Job repeatedly addressed God, while the friends never made any appeal whatsoever on behalf of Job to the God whom they were defending.

It is also necessary to address the implications of the speaking "the truth" or "rightly." What Job had said *to* God was *nekhonah*, possibly both in his choice of "Addressee" and in its content and that would include his accusations, challenges, and curses. Job's barrage of anger was the painful truth about his circumstances, and it was rightly spoken to God. This declaration (42:7–8) is particularly interesting in light of God's apparent rebuke of Job in 40:8–14. There, God challenged Job's audacity in putting *God* on trial and summoned Job to an impossible task, namely, to exercise the same power as God and thus be God's equal. This came after rehearsing at length evidence of God's wisdom and majesty as sovereign Master of the Universe (chap. 38–39). Job was unquestionably put in his place and the reader initially squirms on behalf of Job. Nevertheless, the echoes of Psalm 8:5–6 in this passage are not to be ignored. Perhaps God was reminding Job of his position as God's image bearer and this was an invitation to engage more fully in exploration and governance of the wildness and sublime nature of God's created order. Job's sole focus on the issue of God's justice was demonstrated to be only one small lens; there was much more at stake.[33]

Returning to Job 42:7–8, one further matter is related to our quest. God himself took responsibility for potentially doing something in the realm of folly if prayer and sacrifice did not intervene. Most modern translations shift the "folly" to the friends[34] but that is not the structure of the Hebrew. A literal translation reads "in order not to do with you folly [disgrace]."[35] And this "folly" would have been the punishment of well-meaning defenders of God's justice. It seems that their lives were at risk because of the way they had spoken. It is as if *they* had cursed God and would die unless Job mediated for them.[36]

# THEOLOGICAL IMPLICATIONS— PRAYER AND LIFE

Now, what conclusions can we draw from the wisdom literature? An over-arching factor seems to be the grounded reality of a covenant relationship in which bold trust, bold obedience, and bold fear of the Lord are determinative no matter if the "prayer" is accusation, plea, intercession, or confession.

## Proverbs—Fear of the Lord

Prayers of the righteous person whose trust and fear of the Lord are deeply etched in his/her character bring delight to the Lord. Implicit in that delight is that God *responds*, just as God responds to sacrifice given from an obedient heart. Those are the components of relationship. Further, there is a sense of justice in the whole enterprise. If God's people turn a deaf ear to the cries of others, God will not hear their cries. When God's people are hypocrites, the relationship is false.

Both the direct as well as oblique references to prayer in Proverbs illustrate the dialectic between the cosmological and anthropological emphases that we see with wisdom in Proverbs. On the one hand, humans bear the responsibility for their choices and on the other; there is the profound sense that "God disposes."[37]

## Job—Fear and Prayer

In a horrible irony, God proudly pointed to Job as one who feared God, but Job would declare that *what* he had feared had come upon him. It seems that he had lived his life in dread of unwittingly displeasing God. Perhaps he chose to cover his bets by habitual sacrifice on behalf of his children (1:5)—sacrifice in conjunction with prayer. That was so until the crisis. From the center of the crucible, Job was emboldened to plead for his own death, to call God to justice, and to demand to "see" God—and he did. In the end, Job "came forth as gold" (23:10) refined and chastened, but no longer cowering in fear of an ambiguous unknown.

For their part, Job's friends admonished him to fear the Lord—or else! They talked solely to Job about God in the most pious terms, advising him to pray to God in repentance lest the dismal fate of the wicked in a moral universe overtake him as well. As Job's words continue to tumble forth, it is clear that his principle suffering came from the *people* around him who misunderstood him.[38] To repeat: the friends never appealed on behalf of Job to God. Job, on the other hand, talked frankly about God as he attempted to understand the horror that had overtaken him, but he also appealed again and again to God, evidence of his prior intimate experience with God.[39] It was this long-standing character trait of Job that lay behind God's response to Eliphaz, part of which was the call for Job to intercede for the friends, just as he had done for his children.

## RELEVANCE FOR THE COMMUNITY OF FAITH

Let us take potential life applications one-step further. What must God's people be *doing* in response to reading/hearing these challenges? First, let us examine our seasons of prayer and worship to make absolutely certain that neither of them is contaminated by hypocrisy. Prayer *must* be accompanied by upright lives. Fear, trust, obey, and *pray* that God will keep us far from sins of deceit and self-sufficiency. From Qoheleth comes a clarion warning: If we are offering lots of empty words and making half-hearted vows, best to stop. Period.

By way of contrast, Job offered lots of words as well—but they were not empty. God's endorsement of Job's words to God and about God silences those who are squeamish about articulating ugly truths about life in our fallen world. Of greater import, the honest confrontation of ambiguity, fear, and injustice occurs only in a personal relationship. It is imperative that we nurture our relationships with God, even when God seems unwilling to respond. That means continued, persistent communication—hearing and speaking—depending on God's covenant precious promises. Prayer is the best nourishment for that relationship. Sometimes it is simply the discipline of the action—a good Proverbs concept—as we wrestle with the implications of pain and dread. Job's expressed anguish and his refusal to back down were what prompted the unparalleled revelation of God in the whirlwind.

Before Job interceded for his friends, the "community" was still fractured. It was their sacrifice and Job's prayer, both commanded by God that began a series of restorations for Job's family and friends on the human level. The highest calling of the church is prayer and prayerful worship;

it is the way we best love our neighbors "as ourselves." In fact, "neighbor" in the prayer context takes on global proportions. As with Job, our intercessory ministries are the most critical component. And perhaps, just as the prayer of the suffering Job was efficacious, our most effective pray-ers will be those whose suffering goes past words, but resonates deeply in our hearts—and in the heart of God, who responds by appearing.

We close with a dangerous invitation to join Job–yes, suffering Job. Let us be willing to join him in hammering down the door of heaven in regard to heinous evil and to be willing to pray out of our suffering for the healing of others whose plight, often unknown this side of heaven, may be worse than ours.

---

1. James L. Crenshaw, *Old Testament Wisdom: An Introduction* (Atlanta: John Knox, 1981), 24. See also Walter Brueggemann, *In Man We Trust: the Neglected Side of Biblical Faith* (Richmond: John Knox, 1972), 20–28.

2. Samuel E. Balentine, *Prayer in the Hebrew Bible: The Drama of Divine-Human Dialogue,* OBT (Minneapolis: Fortress Press, 1993), 30.

3. Ibid., 31.

4. Ibid,, 7.

5. Ibid., 145–147. In regard to the power of prayer to reorder chaos, see also Carol A. Newsom, *The Book of Job: A Contest of Moral Imaginations* (Oxford: Oxford University Press, 2003), 127.

6. Balentine, *Prayer in the Hebrew Bible,* 38–39.

7. Ibid., *Prayer in the Hebrew Bible,* 155–156.

8. See Brueggemann, *In Man We Trust,* 22—wisdom's teachers do not use prayer as a means of "passing along our responsibilities to God."

9. William P. Brown, *Character in Crisis: A Fresh Approach to the Wisdom Literature of the Old Testament* (Grand Rapids: William B. Eerdmans, 1996), 120–121.

10. All translations, unless otherwise noted, are the author's. In relation to this verse, see also verses 9 and 26, both of which speak of the Lord detesting the wicked (their sacrifice, way, and thoughts) while he is pleased with those who are pure, upright, and pursue righteousness.

11. See also 19:21, 21:2 and 21:30.

12. "Qoheleth never addresses God in dialogue; either in prayer or lament" (Crenshaw, *Old Testament Wisdom,* 138).

13. Brown, *Character in Crisis,* 120–121.

14. Even Eliphaz acknowledged Job's practice of intercession (22:29–30) in the midst of the stinging condemnation of Job's social lapses (Newsom, *Contest of Moral Imaginations,* 114).

15. This is the only place this Hebrew root (*s-l-d*) appears in the Hebrew Bible, and it is difficult to determine a specific meaning.

16. James Crenshaw, "Murder without Cause: Job," in *A Whirlpool of Torment: Israelite Traditions of God as an Oppressive Presence* (Atlanta: Society of Biblical Literature, 2008), 61.

17. Newsom, *Contest of Moral Imaginations*, 136–138.

18. Choon-Leong Seow, *Job 1–21: Interpretation and Commentary* (Grand Rapids: Eerdmans, 2013), 647–649.

19. Ibid., 736.

20. Newsom, *Contest of Moral Imaginations*, 109–115; 157–159.

21. Newsom's way of expressing this is to say that the friends counseled Job to exercise "moral technology" to set things right (*Contest of Moral Imaginations*, 128).

22. Leo G. Perdue, *Wisdom and Creation: The Theology of Wisdom Literature* (Nashville: Abingdon Press, 1994), 138–139.

23. Seow, *Job 1–21*, 699–700.

24. Newsom, *Contest of Moral Imaginations*, 210–211.

25. Ibid., 155–159.

26. Balentine, *Prayer in the Hebrew Bible*, 172–3.

27. See John Hartley, *The Book of Job*, NICOT (Grand Rapids: Eerdmans, 1988), 535; and E. Dhorme, *A Commentary on the Book of Job*, trans. Harold Knight (Camden: Thomas Nelson and Sons, 1967), 646. The second position is radically stated by John Briggs Curtis, "On Job's Response to Yahweh," *JBL* 98 (1979): 497–511.

28. Balentine, *Prayer in the Hebrew Bible*, 179–180.

29. In regard to the material that follows, see also Elaine Phillips, "Speaking Truthfully: Job's Friends and Job," *Bulletin for Biblical Research* 18.1 (2008): 31–43.

30. Note as representative examples, the NIV, NASB, ESV, KJV, JPS, NRSV.

31. BDB, 39–40; HALOT, 50.

32. Samuel E. Balentine, *Job*, in SHBC, ed. Mark K. McElroy (Macon, Georgia: Smyth & Helwys, 2006), 679–682. Alternatively, based on the apparent anger expressed by God (40:2,8–14), Longman is not inclined to view Job's speeches as paradigmatic for prayers in the midst of suffering. Tremper Longman III, *Job*, in BCOT, ed. Tremper Longman III (Grand Rapids: Baker Books, 2012), 451–453.

33. ASV, NASB, RSV, HCSB, and NIV are representative. The NIV reads "…not deal with you according to your folly."

34. The JPS translation reads "not deal with you vilely…" Dhorme softened the implication of *nevalah* to "disgrace," translating the phrase "not inflicting on you any disgrace…" (*Job*, 648).

35. Norman C. Habel, *The Book of Job*, OTL (Philadelphia: Westminster, 1985), 34.

36. Perdue, *Wisdom and Creation*, 97–98.

37. René Girard, "Job as Failed Scapegoat," in *The Voice from the Whirlwind: Interpreting the Book of Job*, edited by Leo G. Perdue and W. Clark Gilpin (Nashville: Abingdon, 1992), 187.

38. Francis I. Andersen, *Job: An Introduction and Commentary*, TOTC (London: InterVarsity, 1976), 97–98, 221, noted this distinctive, stating that it makes Job the only "authentic theologian in the book." See also Dale Patrick, "Job's Address of God," *ZAW* 91 (1979): 269.

# Prayer in Ruth and Esther

## Brittany D. Kim

When seeking to develop a theology of prayer, the books of Ruth and Esther would not immediately come to mind since they contain no standard prayers of petition or thanksgiving (however, see below for a discussion of the additions to Esther found in the Septuagint). Ruth, however, is punctuated throughout by frequent invocations of blessing. Although typically addressed to the intended recipient of the blessing, rather than to God,[1] they are nevertheless a form of prayer, implicitly calling on God to enact the pronounced benediction.[2] As Sabine Van Den Eynde puts it, blessing someone involves "saying words of which the effectuation is in God's power only."[3] Yet the relevance of Ruth and Esther for a theology of prayer goes beyond Ruth's contribution to a biblical understanding of blessing. Precisely because they fail to offer any prayers of petition in the midst of desperate situations, these books may have something to say to others who face similarly dark circumstances where it seems like God is absent and perhaps unreachable by prayer. Thus, after examining the blessing formulae in Ruth, we will explore the significance of this absence of prayer by focusing on the narrative portrayals of God, Naomi, and Esther and concluding with some observations about faith, prayer, and the actions of God.

## BLESSING FORMULAE IN RUTH

The centrality of blessing to the book of Ruth is demonstrated by the nine distinct acts of blessing contained in the book's four short chapters. Although only five of these occurrences employ the Hebrew term *barakh*, meaning "to bless," the other four instances clearly adhere to the biblical pattern, effecting the same speech act as those that do use the terminology.[4] The blessings vary in form, purpose, and significance, thus demonstrating how blessing can be applied to a variety of situations.

# RUTH 1: NAOMI AND HER DAUGHTERS-IN-LAW

Blessing first emerges in the book when the bereaved Naomi prepares to return from her sojourn in Moab to the land of Israel and attempts to send her widowed daughters-in-law back to their maternal households, declaring, "May Yahweh deal with you faithfully (khesed), as you have dealt with the dead and with me. May Yahweh grant that you should find rest, each in the house of her husband" (1:8b–9a).[5] Naomi's blessing arises out of gratitude and a feeling of indebtedness for the devotion that her daughters-in-law have shown to her and her family.[6] Since she has no resources to return the favor, she articulates her thankfulness and calls on Yahweh to repay her debt by demonstrating the same faithfulness to them. Her words also draw their relationship to a positive conclusion, releasing her daughters-in-law from any further obligation toward her.[7] The second part of Naomi's blessing specifies how Yahweh may extend faithfulness to her daughters-in-law—by granting them the "rest" (or "security") that she herself lacks in her vulnerable position as a widow without any male protector.[8]

# RUTH 2: THE INTRODUCTION OF BOAZ

The next blessing formulae appear in 2:4 where Boaz says to his reapers, "May Yahweh be with you," and they reply, "May Yahweh bless (barakh) you." Although these brief addresses could be taken simply as standardized greetings, lacking the force of a true blessing, the first constitutes part of the narrative introduction of Boaz, which highlights his piety and concern for others.[9] Thus, his words should be seen as a genuine blessing, which seeks to elicit Yahweh's ongoing presence and favor for the other party in the midst of everyday life.[10] Boaz's subsequent blessing of Ruth in 2:12 reaffirms Naomi's earlier words to her daughters-in-law, declaring,

"May Yahweh repay your deed, and may your reward be complete from Yahweh, the God of Israel, under whose wings you have come to seek refuge."[11] Although he does not speak out of personal gratitude, Boaz acknowledges Ruth's faithfulness to Naomi (v. 11), perhaps reflecting a corporate gratitude for the foreigner's kindness toward one of his own people. Then, like Naomi, he hands Ruth over to Yahweh's care.

When Ruth returns to Naomi with an abundance of grain, her mother-in-law asks where she gleaned, exclaiming, "May the man who took notice of you be blessed" (barukh—2:19). After learning the identity of this man, she again declares, "Blessed (barukh) be he by Yahweh, who has not forsaken his faithfulness (khesed) with the living or the dead" (2:20a). As in 1:8–9, Naomi's blessings are borne out of gratefulness, in this case for Boaz's generous provision for Ruth and herself, which also reflects a kind consideration for their deceased husbands.[12] Here, however, Naomi's blessing remains general, without any further elaboration of what it should entail.[13] This difference may be due to Naomi's greater intimacy with Ruth's situation; she may not know how Yahweh's blessing would be of most benefit to Boaz.

# RUTH 3–4: THE MARRIAGE OF BOAZ AND RUTH

Ruth's nighttime rendezvous with Boaz in chapter 3 prompts him to invoke a second blessing on her: "Blessed (brukhah) be you by Yahweh, my daughter. You have made your last act of faithfulness (khesed) better than the first in not going after young men, whether poor or rich" (v. 10). Once again Boaz commends Ruth to Yahweh in acknowledgement of her devotion toward Naomi. Not only did she leave her homeland to follow her mother-in-law (see 2:11–12), but she now seeks a marriage with Boaz—rather than with any of the eligible young men who may possess more personal attractions—in an attempt to secure the redemption of the family land and provide an heir for Naomi.[14]

The final two blessings in the book come from the townspeople. When Boaz redeems Ruth at the city gate, "all the people at the gate and the elders" pronounce a three-fold blessing, "May Yahweh make the woman who is coming into your house like Rachel and Leah, who together built up the house of Israel, and may you prosper ('aseh-khayil) in Ephrathah and [your] name be called (*qra'-shem*) in Bethlehem.[15] And may your house be like the house of Perez, whom Tamar bore to Judah, due to the offspring that Yahweh will give you by this young woman" (4:11–12). Although this blessing comes immediately after Boaz publicly accepts the role of kinsman-redeemer, it does not stem from an acknowledgement of his kindness toward Ruth. Instead, it functions as a standard marriage blessing, calling on Yahweh to bless Boaz's soon-to-be wife, himself, and his house by bestowing fertility, wealth, and honor on the new couple.[16]

After a brief comment that the consummation of the marriage does indeed produce the hoped-for offspring (v. 13), the theme of blessing culminates in the praise expressed by the town's women, who declare to Naomi, "Blessed (*barukh*) be Yahweh, who has not left you without a redeemer today, and may his name be called in Israel" (v. 14). In this case, the blessing functions as a public declaration of Yahweh's goodness, expressed in his provision for Naomi.[17] The specified redeemer is identified by v. 15 not as the expected Boaz, but as Ruth's newborn son, who "will be to [Naomi] a restorer of life and a sustainer of [her] old age."[18]

Since the first part of the blessing extols Yahweh for his kindness to Naomi, the second part—"may his name be called (*yiqqare' shmo*) in Israel"—could express the desire that Yahweh's name would be lifted up in praise. Alternatively, it may wish for the renown of the "redeemer," who provides the nearest antecedent. In that case, v. 14b would echo the people's blessing of Boaz in v. 11, increasing the range of the child's fame beyond that of his father—from Bethlehem to all of Israel.[19] Perhaps it is not necessary to choose between these options. The ambiguity may be intentional, and the book fulfills both aims, extolling Yahweh for his gracious deliverance of Naomi and perpetuating the name of her grandson, Obed.

# TOWARD A BIBLICAL THEOLOGY OF BLESSING

Coming at significant junctures in the book of Ruth, the blessings provide commentary on the movement of the story and the actions of its major characters. Against the background of loss and despair that marks the story's beginning, they stand out in stark relief, painting a portrait of Yahweh as a God who providentially supports and sustains his own people, as well as those foreigners who have acted faithfully toward them. Some invoke Yahweh's presence and provision in the mundane events (2:4) or momentous occasions of life (4:11–12), while others arise out of personal gratitude or an acknowledgment of a person's praiseworthy deeds (1:8–9; 2:12, 19–20; 3:10). The latter type of blessing brings recognition and honor to the recipient and implicitly asks Yahweh to repay that person for their meritorious actions. The climactic blessing of Yahweh in 4:14 is a variation of this type of blessing. Although no one can repay Yahweh, the women of Bethlehem do all that is in their power to recognize what he has done, eliciting honor and praise.

The fact that blessings are found in the mouth of virtually every character in the book, except Ruth the Moabite, suggests that all of God's people—regardless of gender, position, or status—have the authority to pronounce blessings.[20] Moreover, the power of blessing is demonstrated by the fulfillment of many of the book's benedictions in the narrative resolution involving Ruth's marriage to Boaz and the birth of a child. Thus the book provides a model for how God's people today may effectually invoke God's providential care in the lives of those around them. By offering blessings, we may go beyond merely wishing others well and actually invite God's gracious presence into their lives. Blessing can also provide us with a means of truly thanking those whose kindness we can never repay by asking God to pour out his favor on them. And finally, in blessing God we may publicly express the depth of our gratitude for the overwhelming generosity he has shown us.

# THE ABSENCE OF PRAYER IN RUTH

Although Naomi invokes Yahweh's name to bless both her daughters-in-law and Boaz (1:8–9; 2:20), she never turns to Yahweh to cry out for help in her distress. Her failure to plead with God for redemption ties in with the book's larger portrayal of divine activity.

# CHARACTERIZATION OF GOD

Throughout the book of Ruth, Yahweh remains hidden, operating behind the scenes by (1) ending the famine that had plagued Israel (1:6), (2) leading Ruth to glean in the field of a kinsman-redeemer (2:3), and

(3) allowing Ruth to conceive (4:13). There are no miraculous displays of his mighty power, so only those who are closely attuned to his presence will recognize the signs of his hand at work. In each of these instances, the text employs different tactics to clue the reader in to Yahweh's activity: (1) unidentified informants tell Naomi that Yahweh has brought food to Israel; (2) The narrator suggestively states that Ruth "happened by chance upon the portion of the field belonging to Boaz;" And finally, (3) the narrator clearly reveals that "Yahweh gave (*vayyitten*) [Ruth] conception," bringing the theme of Yahweh's involvement in the story to its climax.[21] Yet even here, Yahweh does not act solely on his own initiative but rather fulfills the blessing pronounced by the people concerning "the offspring that Yahweh [would] give (*yitten*) [Boaz] by this young woman" (4:12b).[22]

Moreover, Yahweh frequently acts by means of the human characters. Indeed, human action is often central to the fulfillment of the blessings, a point that is emphasized by subtle verbal connections.[23] For example, Naomi's blessing on Ruth asks that Yahweh would treat her with "faithfulness" (*khesed*) and provide her with "rest" (*menukhah*—1:8–9). Her request is largely fulfilled, however, through the "faithfulness" (*khesed*) shown by Boaz (2:20) and Naomi's own attempt to "seek rest" (*manoakh*) for Ruth by instructing her to pay a nighttime visit to Boaz (3:1). A similar point may be made in 2:20. Although Naomi undoubtedly intends to say that Boaz "has not forsaken his faithfulness (*khesed*) with the living or the dead," the grammatical ambiguity concerning whether the subject is Boaz or Yahweh may be intentional on the part of the author. Certainly Yahweh demonstrates his own "faithfulness" (*khesed*) to Ruth and Naomi through that of Boaz.[24]

Boaz also expresses a wish that Ruth would receive her due reward from Yahweh, "under whose wings (*khnaphim*) [she] has come to take refuge" (2:12), but his blessing is realized through his own response to her request, "Spread your wing (*khanaph*) [i.e., cloak] over your servant, for you are a kinsman-redeemer" (3:9).[25] As Tamara Cohn Eskanazi and Tikva Frymer-Kensky observe, the book centers "on ordinary human beings whose actions bring God's presence into the world."[26] Through human invocations of blessing and acts of faithfulness, divine blessing ultimately triumphs over "the curses of famine, exile, and death."[27]

Yahweh providentially cares for Naomi's needs through the devotion of Ruth, the kindness of Boaz, and the gift of a grandson.

# CHARACTERIZATION OF NAOMI

The affirmation of Yahweh's care and concern implicitly evoked by the book's many blessings forms a striking contrast with Naomi's anguished cry in 1:20–21: "Do not call me Naomi [i.e., Pleasant]; call me Mara [i.e., Bitter], for the Almighty has dealt very bitterly with me. I went away full, but Yahweh has brought me back empty. Why call me Naomi, since Yahweh has testified against me, and the Almighty has brought disaster upon me."[28] Noting intertextual resonances with Job, as well as with complaints made by Moses (Exod. 5:22–23; Num. 11:11) and Elijah (1 Kings 17:20), Katharine Doob Sakenfeld ponders why Naomi's words are not addressed directly to God as in these other similar texts. In response, she poses the rhetorical question, "If Naomi supposes God will hear her words of concern and blessing [e.g., in 1:8–9], why should she not hope that God will hear (or at least overhear) her cry as well?" Thus she terms Naomi's cry an "implicit 'prayer' or prayer 'in the process of formation,'" noting that "although the depth of complaint found in Jeremiah's laments and in some psalms suggests that there is nothing we cannot say to God, it is still true that many people find it easier to express their most vehement protests to other people rather than directly to God."[29]

Perhaps, however, Naomi's failure to address God reflects not so much a reticence to voice her "most vehement protests . . . directly to God" but rather a complete lack of faith that he will intervene on her behalf. According to the narrator, Naomi returns to Israel because she "had heard in the fields of Moab that Yahweh had visited his people to give them food" (1:6), which suggests that she recognizes Yahweh's provision for her people. Moreover, the blessing she pronounces on her daughters-in-law reveals some level of belief that Yahweh should be concerned about her relatives and that he has the power to act even in Moab, the land of Chemosh.[30] However, in that blessing she classifies herself with the dead rather than with her daughters-in-law, who may find new life through Yahweh's blessing.[31] Furthermore, when her daughters-in-law initially refuse to leave her, she declares, "It is more bitter for me than for you, for the hand of Yahweh has gone out against me" (1:13b). Since, in her perspective, Yahweh has deliberately set himself against her, she sees no glimmer of hope that anything can change her desolate situation.

Indeed, as Naomi tells the women of the village, not only has Yahweh "brought disaster upon" her, but he has also "testified against" her (1:20b–21). Sakenfeld is right to observe that Naomi's statement does not imply acceptance of guilt. As with Job, it seems more likely that "divine action in the life of Naomi is bitter . . . precisely because it is so utterly inexplicable."[32] Nevertheless, unlike Job, Naomi offers no resistance against her fate. As a vulnerable widow, powerless to execute justice for herself in the human realm, she may feel that she has no recourse when Yahweh, "the Almighty" (*Shadday*), has acted as a prosecuting witness against her.[33] Whatever the reason for her passivity, the text gives no indication that Naomi expects Yahweh to hear or respond to her complaint.[34]

Although some scholars see Naomi as reversing her negative assessment of Yahweh in Ruth 2:20,[35] as noted above, her praise of one "who has not forsaken his faithfulness with the living or the dead" is more likely directed toward Boaz. After the birth of her grandson, the women of the town erupt in praise for Yahweh's provision of a redeemer (4:14–15), but Naomi remains strangely silent. Thus, nowhere in the book does she offer a more positive evaluation of Yahweh's actions toward herself.[36] Nevertheless, the women's climactic words decisively overturn Naomi's earlier complaint, drawing a clear verbal connection. Whereas Naomi lamented that Yahweh had "brought [her] back (Hiphil *shuv*) empty" (1:21), the women declare that her grandson "will be to [her] a restorer (Hiphil *shuv*) of life" (4:15).[37] Presumably Naomi will now find comfort and healing in the embrace of her new grandson (4:16) and rest in the care of her son-in-law.[38]

# THE ABSENCE OF PRAYER IN ESTHER

Whereas Naomi languishes under the effects of personal tragedy, the book of Esther presents the large-scale threat of genocide to the Jews living under Persian rule. Throughout the kingdom, Jews respond to the news of their coming annihilation with "great mourning," accompanied by "fasting (*tsum*) and weeping (*bkhi*) and wailing (*misped*)" while lying on "sackcloth and ashes" (Esth. 4:3). Similarly, Esther's uncle Mordecai dons "sackcloth and ashes," after tearing "his garments" (*qara' bgadim*), and cries out "with a great and bitter cry" (v. 1). Strikingly absent, however, is any mention of prayer.

An intertextual connection between Esther 4:3 and Joel 2:12–14a may suggest that the purpose of the Jews' fasting is to demonstrate repentance in order to elicit Yahweh's deliverance: " 'But even now,' declares Yahweh, 'return to me with all your heart and with fasting (*tsum*) and weeping (*bkhi*) and wailing (*misped*) and tear (*qara*) your heart and not your garments (*bgadim*).' Now return to Yahweh your God, for he is gracious and compassionate, slow to anger and abounding in steadfast love; and he relents over calamity. Who knows whether he will not turn and relent and leave behind a blessing?"[39] Any allusion to repentance, however, is veiled at best. Esther 4:3 describes the actions of the Jews merely as expressions of mourning.[40]

When Mordecai informs Esther of the situation of the Jews and convinces her to risk death by approaching the king to plead for the lives of her people, she instructs Mordecai to "gather all the Jews who may be found in Susa and fast (*tsum*) for her for three days while she and her maidens do the same. At the end of the three days, she will go to the king and appeal for mercy" (4:16). Since this fast serves to prepare Esther for her risky endeavor, it may aim to entreat God's favor on her behalf.[41] Yet even here there is surprisingly no explicit reference to prayer.[42]

# THE SEPTUAGINT ADDITIONS

This absence of prayer was seen by some early transmitters of the text as a glaring omission, as is clear from a comparison of the Hebrew and Greek versions of Esther. In the Septuagint, Mordecai's initial request that Esther intervene with the king is prefaced with the instruction, "Call upon the Lord" (4:8 NETS).[43] Moreover, one of six additions inserted into the Greek version recounts the prayers Mordecai and Esther offer before Esther's rendezvous with the king.[44] Mordecai's prayer (vv. 2–10) acknowledges the Lord's greatness and explains Mordecai's failure to bow to Haman, which provoked the genocidal edict (Esth. 3:1–6), as an act of piety. Finally, it pleads with the Lord to preserve his people so that they may continue to praise him.

Esther prepares herself to seek the Lord's favor by donning garments of mourning and "cover[ing] her head with ashes and dung" (v. 13).[45] In her prayer, which is considerably longer than Mordecai's (vv. 14b–30), Esther first notes her utter dependence on the Lord and recollects his election of Israel. She then attributes her people's current subjugation to their sin in worshiping idols but complains that their oppressors now seek "to stop the mouths of those who praise you and to extinguish the glory of your house and your altar" (v. 20 NETS). Thus she pleads, "do not surrender your scepter to those who don't exist" (v. 22 NETS), imploring the Lord as sovereign King over all to give her courage, change the king's heart, and deliver his people.[46] Finally Esther describes how she loathes her position as Persian queen and refuses to eat the king's defiled food, concluding with one last petition for deliverance.

Both prayers resemble other petitionary prayers and laments found in the OT, which often ground their entreaties in Yahweh's sovereignty (Isa. 37:16; Ps. 74:12–17) or concern for Israel (Pss. 44:1–8 [MT. vv. 2–9]; 74:2; Isa. 63:7–9), sometimes calling on God to rescue his people for his own sake (Pss. 44:26 [MT. v 27]; 79:9–10; Isa. 37:20; Dan. 9:17–19). Moreover, Esther's prayer reflects the common biblical practice of offering a corporate confession of sin before requesting God's deliverance (see esp. Dan. 9:4–15; also Ps. 79:8–9; Neh. 1:6–7).[47]

There is certainly much to be gained from a detailed study of these prayers. For example, they emphasize the sovereignty of God over even the greatest earthly powers,[48] and they may challenge the contemporary people of God to adopt a more God-centered approach in their own prayers of petition, rooting their requests in God's character and concerns rather than solely in their own needs or desires. Moreover, the Greek text of Esther suggests that in the most perilous situations the first and primary recourse of God's people should be to seek him in prayer, trusting in his intervention.[49] However, both the Jewish and Protestant Christian communities have accepted the Hebrew form of the text as canonical, and that version offers a significantly different perspective on prayer, which emerges more clearly through an examination of how the book portrays the workings of God and the character of Esther.

# CHARACTERIZATION OF GOD

One of the most striking and frequently noted features of the book of Esther is that it makes no reference to God. This omission, however, does not mean that God is entirely absent. The clearest indication of God's presence comes in Esther 4:14, where Mordecai declares to Esther, "For if you keep silent at this time, relief and deliverance will arise for the Jews from another place, but you and your father's house will perish. And who knows whether you have come to royalty for such a time as this?" The simplest explanation of Mordecai's assurance that the Jews will be delivered from their plight is that he trusts in God's protection of his people.[50] Moreover, his suggestion that Esther may have arisen to her current position "for such a time as this" probably alludes to God's providential hand guiding the events of her life up to this point. Thus Mordecai hints that if Esther refuses to play the role for which she has been prepared, God will find another means of achieving the same end.[51]

Within the narrative, the hand of God may be discerned in the "favor" Esther receives in the sight of both people (2:15) and king (2:17; 5:2; cf. Gen. 39:21), which leads to her accession to the throne and secures the king's mercy when she approaches him unbidden.[52] God's hidden providence may also be identified behind the book's many coincidences. Most notably, the turning point of the story comes when the king has a bout of insomnia and listens to his servants read from the court chronicles. They happen upon the account of Mordecai overturning a plot to assassinate the king, which prompts the king to honor Mordecai on the same day that Haman sought to have him executed (6:1–4), thus putting into motion Mordecai's rise and Haman's fall. The fact that Mordecai heard the plot against the king (2:19–23) is also a remarkable "chance" occurrence, as are the sudden departure of the former queen (1:10–22), the lot for the day of destruction falling on the most distant month (3:7), and Haman's ill-timed entreaty for mercy from Queen Esther (7:7–8). Taken together, all these suggestive comments and fortuitous circumstances point toward the hidden workings of God, through which he carefully orchestrates events to bring about salvation for his people.[53]

# CHARACTERIZATION OF ESTHER

Ultimately God's deliverance comes through the bold intervention of Esther, but until chapter 4 Esther remains an entirely passive character, allowing her circumstances to shape her identity as a Persian woman and wife of the king.[54] When she is swept up into the king's harem, the text offers no indication that she tries to escape or oppose her fate or even that she deplores it.[55] Her lack of self-assertion is particularly striking when contrasted with the book of Daniel, which also describes the situation of Israelite exiles in a foreign court. Whereas Daniel refuses to "defile himself with the king's food or wine" and requests that he be given only vegetables and water (Dan. 1:8, 12), Esther apparently offers no resistance when given her "portion of food" (Esth. 2:9b). Like Daniel, Esther also obtains the "affection" or "devotion" (*khesed*) of the eunuch who has charge over her (Esth. 2:9a; cf. Dan. 1:9). Thus, had she asked, she too might have been granted special concessions. In submission to Mordecai, however, she conceals her identity as a Jew (Esth. 2:10).

So removed is Esther from the situation of her people that she is not even aware of the king's edict authorizing their annihilation, despite her residence within the court (4:5).[56] When Mordecai informs her of the plight of the Jews and attempts to press her into their service, she is initially reluctant to intervene since seeking an audience with the king could result in her death (vv. 6–11). Only after Mordecai warns her that she faces destruction if she remains silent does she choose to act, but her transformation is instantaneous and remarkable.[57] Rejecting the privilege and abundance that characterize life in the Persian court, marked by the book's frequent references to feasting, she now joins the Jews in their fasting.[58] She also adopts a leadership role, issuing commands to her guardian and her people, and she courageously accepts the possibility that death awaits her, declaring, "I will go to the king, though it is against the law; and if I perish, I perish" (v. 16b).[59]

Esther does not, however, offer any hint of faith in God's intervention on her behalf. Once again a comparison with the book of Daniel is instructive. When Shadrach, Meshach, and Abednego face a more certain death by failing to bow before Nebuchadnezzar's golden image, they say, "Our God whom we serve is able to deliver us from the burning fiery furnace, and he will deliver us from your hand, O king. But if not, let it be known to you, O king, that we will not serve your gods or pay homage to the golden image you have erected" (Dan. 3:17–18). They too courageously embrace their fate should no help come their way, but unlike Esther, they affirm that God has the power to rescue them and even express faith that "he will deliver [them]." By contrast, Esther does not even imitate Mordecai in commenting obliquely on God's providence. Thus, whether her request that the Jews fast for her implies an appeal for prayer or merely reflects her identification with Jewish religious practice, it does not convey any confidence in God's response.[60] The narrative ambiguity concerning the purpose of the fast may mirror Esther's religious uncertainty.

## CONCLUSION: FAITH, PRAYER, AND THE ACTIONS OF GOD

The absence of any prayers of petition in the books of Ruth and Esther coheres with the narrative portrayals of Naomi and Esther as lacking faith that God will act to overturn their dire situations. Nevertheless, despite any unambiguous attempts to solicit God's involvement, both books portray God as active behind the scenes, ultimately bringing about deliverance for his people.[61] Therefore, these books offer hope to people today that find themselves in similarly desperate circumstances and perceive God as too distant or unconcerned to be moved by prayer. Recognizing God's providential guidance at work in the lives of Naomi and Esther may give us the courage and faith to pray for God's intervention when we are overwhelmed by the crushing difficulties of life in a broken world. But even if our doubt is too severe, our despair too deep, or our voice too feeble to break through the deafening chaos and reach out to God, these books may help us to open our eyes to observe any "chance" circumstances that might signal traces of God's hand at work. Perhaps in discerning the faintest glimpses of God's providential care in our own lives, we may take the first steps toward healing and a restored faith.

---

1. Thus they may be distinguished from traditional prayer in one sense (see Sabine Van Den Eynde, "Blessed by God—Blessed Be God: *Eulogeo* and the Concept of Blessing in the LXX with Special Attention to the Book of Ruth," in *Interpreting Translation*, ed. F. García Martínez and M. Vervenne, BETL 192 [Leuven: Leuven University Press, 2005], 424).

2. See Patrick D. Miller, *They Cried to the Lord: The Form and Theology of Biblical Prayer* (Minneapolis: Augsburg Fortress, 1994), 292; Christopher Wright Mitchell, *The Meaning of* brk *"To Bless" in the Old Testament*, SBLDS 95, ed. J.J.M. Roberts (Atlanta: Scholars Press, 1987), 95. Commentators often refer to specific blessings in Ruth as "prayers"; e.g., on Ruth 1:8–9, see Daniel I. Block, *Judges, Ruth*, NAC 6, ed. E. Ray Clendenen (Nashville: Broadman & Holman, 1999), 633; Kirsten Nielsen, *Ruth: A Commentary*, OTL (Louisville: Westminster John Knox Press, 1997), 47; also Michael E. W. Thompson, "New Life Amid the Alien Corn: The Book of Ruth," in *EvQ* 65 (1993): 197–210, who calls all of the book's blessings "prayers" and thus sees prayer as central to the narrative.

3. Van Den Eynde, "Blessed by God," 424. Ruth's curse in 1:17b could also be taken as an implicit prayer: "Thus may Yahweh do to me and more if [even] death divides me from

you." In that case, however, Yahweh's intervention is called for only if Ruth breaks her vow to follow Naomi to the grave.

4. Ibid., 425. On the application of speech-act theory to biblical blessings, see further Mitchell, *Meaning of* brk.

5. All translations mine unless otherwise noted.

6. See further Moshe Greenberg, *Biblical Prose Prayer: As a Window to the Popular Religion of Ancient Israel* (Berkeley: University of California Press, 1983), 33–34.

7. See Katharine Doob Sakenfeld, *The Meaning of Hesed in the Hebrew Bible: A New Inquiry*, in Harvard Semitic Monographs 17, ed. Frank Moore Cass (Missoula: Scholars Press, 1978), 109; Robert L. Hubbard, *The Book of Ruth*, NICOT (Grand Rapids: Eerdmans, 1988), 103.

8. Thompson divides the blessings in Ruth into two categories—prayers of "intercession" and of "thanksgiving" ("New Life," 204–7); however, these categories are somewhat misleading. As Ruth 1:8–9 demonstrates, many of the blessings include elements of both.

9. See Tod Linafelt, "Ruth," in Tod Linafelt and Timothy K. Beal, *Ruth and Esther* (Berit Olam; Collegeville: Liturgical Press, 1999), 29; Mitchell, *Meaning of* brk, 106–7.

10. Miller, *They Cried to the Lord*, 291; also Tamara Cohn Eskenazi and Tikva Frymer-Kensky, *Ruth*, in JPSBC (Philadelphia: JPS, 2011), 31. Boaz's statement that he "commanded the young men not to touch" Ruth (2:9) may, however, raise questions about the character and piety of the reapers. Otherwise, why would such a command be necessary? (Observation noted by Marion Taylor in private communication.) Thus, while the reapers adopt Boaz's style of address, it not clear whether their words entail a serious intention to invoke Yahweh's blessing.

11. Nielsen sees here a suggestive echo of Gen. 15:1, in which Abraham's "reward" involves the promise of a multitude of offspring (*Ruth*, 59).

12. Although the grammar of 2:20 does not specify whether the "faithfulness" Naomi lauds is that of Boaz or Yahweh, the close parallel in 2 Sam. 2:5 favors the former (Basil A. Rebera, "Yahweh or Boaz: Ruth 2:20 Reconsidered," *The Bible Translator* 36 (1985): 317–27; Hubbard, *Ruth*, 186; André LaCocque, *Ruth: A Continental Commentary* (Minneapolis: Augsburg Fortress, 2004), 77–78; contra Nielsen, *Ruth*, 63; Block, *Judges, Ruth*, 673).

13. On this type of blessing, see further Mitchell, *Meaning of* brk, 110–15.

14. Hubbard, *Ruth*, 214.

15. Simon B. Parker argues that *'aseh-khayil* relates to the wish for offspring ("Marriage Blessing in Israelite and Ugaritic Literature," in *JBL* 95 (1976): 23–24, esp. n. 2). Elsewhere, however, the collocation means "to fight valiantly" (1 Sam. 14:48), "to do excellently" (Prov. 31:29), or "to obtain wealth" (Deut 8:18), and the idea of prospering financially makes the most sense in the context of a marriage blessing (Block, *Judges, Ruth*, 723).

16. This blessing may have been a regularly recited local formulation, though readers recognize ironic connections to the specific situation of Boaz and Ruth. See Moshe J. Bernstein, "Two Multivalent Readings in the Ruth Narrative," *JSOT* 50 (1991): 20–25.

17. See further Greenberg, *Biblical Prose Prayer*, 32; also Mitchell, *Meaning of* brk, 155–57; Block, *Judges, Ruth*, 726–27.

18. Eskenazi and Frymer-Kensky, *Ruth*, 89; Hubbard, *Ruth*, 271.

19. Katharine Doob Sakenfeld, *Ruth*, IBC (Louisville: Westminster John Knox, 1999), 82; Block, *Judges, Ruth*, 727–28.

20. Nevertheless, by binding herself to Naomi, Ruth ultimately becomes a source of blessing for her mother-in-law and experiences blessing herself. Thus, the book illustrates Yahweh's

promise to Abraham, "I will bless those who bless you . . . and through you all the families of the earth will be blessed" (Gen. 12:3).

21. Only in 1:6 and 4:13 are positive actions attributed directly to Yahweh, though Naomi also speaks of his actions against her in 1:13 and 1:20–21 (see further below). Elsewhere, the divine name (Yahweh) is invoked only in the blessings (1:8–9; 2:4, 12, 20; 3:10; 4:11–12, 14), Ruth's curse (1:17), and an oath made by Boaz (3:13), while Ruth also mentions "God" ('*Elohim*) in her vow to follow Naomi (1:16; see also 2:12).

22. Miller, *They Cried to the Lord*, 293; the verbal link is noted by Eskenazi and Frymer-Kensky, *Ruth*, 87.

23. See Katharine Doob Sakenfeld, "Naomi's Cry: Reflections on Ruth 1:20–21," in *A God So Near: Essays on Old Testament Theology in Honor of Patrick D. Miller*, ed. Brent A. Strawn and Nancy R. Bowen (Winona Lake: Eisenbrauns, 2003), 141; Thompson, "New Life," 207–8.

24. C. John Collins, "Ambiguity and Theology in Ruth: Ruth 1:21 and 2:20," in *Presb* 19, (1993): 100.

25. See Nielsen, *Ruth*, 59–60; Collins, "Ambiguity and Theology," 100–101.

26. Eskenazi and Frymer-Kensky, *Ruth*, 88.

27. Phyllis Trible, *God and the Rhetoric of Sexuality* (Philadelphia: Fortress, 1978), 195.

28. Sakenfeld, "Naomi's Cry," 130–31.

29. Ibid., 142–43. Linafelt "Ruth," 20 suggests instead that Naomi's silence before Yahweh "may be due to the fact that Naomi—unlike Moses and Elijah, the paradigmatic prophets of the LORD—has never herself been addressed by God nor has she been called by God to some great task," but that would not explain why she acts differently than Job.

30. Block, *Judges, Ruth*, 633.

31. See Danna Nolan Fewell and David Miller Gunn, *Compromising Redemption: Relating Characters in the Book of Ruth* (Eugene: Wipf and Stock, 2009), 71; Linafelt, "Ruth," 10.

32. Sakenfeld, "Naomi's Cry," 136; similarly Collins, "Ambiguity and Theology," 99.

33. For a reading of Naomi's complaint against the social-cultural background of childlessness and widowhood in ancient Israel, see Amelia Devin Freedman, *God as an Absent Character in Biblical Hebrew Narrative: A Literary-Theoretical Study*, Studies in Biblical Literature 82 (New York: Peter Lang, 2005), 141–51. Or perhaps Naomi is so traumatized by the series of tragic events that have befallen her that she is simply incapable of looking beyond her intense and immediate pain to appeal to Yahweh (suggestion made by Marion Taylor in private communication).

34. See also Kristin Moen Saxegaard, *Character Complexity in the Book of Ruth*, FAT 2/47 (Tübingen: Mohr Siebeck, 2010), 92–94.

35. See, e.g., Block, *Judges, Ruth*, 673; Thompson, "New Life," 205.

36. See further Saxegaard, *Character Complexity*, 101–3.

37. Although *shuv* is a key word in the book of Ruth, appearing 15x, it is found in the Hiphil stem only in these two verses. The women also laud Ruth as "better to [Naomi] than seven sons" (4:15b), which suggests that even at the height of her grief Naomi was never truly "empty" (Freedman, *God as an Absent Character*, 149–50), though she failed to acknowledge Ruth in her outcry to the women of the town. See also Danna Nolan Fewell and David M. Gunn, "'A Son Is Born to Naomi': Literary Allusions and Interpretation in the Book of Ruth," in *JSOT* 40 (1988): 100.

38. See further Thompson, "New Life," 202.

39. Karen H. Jobes, *Esther* (Grand Rapids: Zondervan, 1999), 136–37; see also Jonathan Grossman, *Esther: The Outer Narrative and the Hidden Reading*, Siphrut: Literature and Theology of the Hebrew Scriptures 6 (Winona Lake: Eisenbrauns, 2011), 113–14.

40. See also Martin Pröbstle, "Is There a God Behind This Text?: A Closer Look at Esther 4:14 and 16," in *Creation, Life, and Hope*, ed. Jiří Moskala (Berrien Springs: Andrews University, 2000), 163 n.49; David J. A. Clines, *Ezra, Nehemiah, Esther*, NCB (Grand Rapids: Eerdmans, 1984), 302. On the connection of these actions with mourning, see Exod. 12:30; 2 Sam. 1:11–12; 3:31; Jer. 6:26, 49:3.

41. Grossman, *Esther*, 122; Pröbstle, "Is There a God," 163; Carey A. Moore, *Esther: Introduction, Translation, and Notes* AB 7b (New York: Doubleday, 1971), 51.

42. Elsewhere in the OT fasting is linked with the language of "seeking" (*biqqesh* or *darash*) God (2 Sam. 12:16 [cf. vv. 21–23]; 2 Chr. 20:3; Ezra 8:21, 23; Dan. 9:3), "praying" (*hithpallel* or the noun form *tephillah*—Neh. 1:4; Ps. 35:13; Dan. 9:3), "crying out" (*za'aq*) to Yahweh" (Joel 1:14), and negatively, Yahweh failing to "hear" (*shama'*) his people (Isa. 58:3–4; Jer. 14:12). Ronald W. Pierce suggests that the omission of any reference to prayer in Esther 4 is intended to convey that prayers were not offered, in keeping with what he sees as the book's depiction of Jewish secularization under Persian rule ("The Politics of Esther and Mordecai: Courage or Compromise?," *BBR* 2 (1992): 87–88), but he does not explain the purpose of the fast called by Esther. As will be suggested below, the ambiguity concerning Esther's fast may be intentional.

43. Another early Greek translation, the Alpha-text, also alters Esther's concluding words to Mordecai. Rather than calling for a fast, she declares, "Proclaim a religious service, and petition God earnestly" (v. 11 NETS, corresponding to MT v. 16).

44. Known as Addition C, this insertion is found between chap. 4 and 5.

45. On the significance of Esther's bodily humiliation as a sign of obeisance to the divine King, see Esther Menn, "Prayer of the Queen: Esther's Religious Self in the Septuagint," in *Religion and the Self in Antiquity*, ed. David Brakke, Michael L. Satlow, and Steven Weitzman (Bloomington: Indiana University Press, 2005), 81.

46. As Menn observes, "God's own honor and power" are imperiled by the Persian king's edict (Ibid., 74).

47. The personal apologies of Mordecai and Esther (vv. 5–7, 26–29), however, are somewhat surprising in a communal prayer of petition. These verses are undoubtedly aimed at demonstrating the moral and spiritual rectitude of these characters in the face of ambiguities in the Hebrew text, defending Mordecai against the allegation of pride and Esther against the charges of wantonly marrying a Gentile and breaking the food laws (Jon D. Levenson, *Esther: A Commentary*, in OTL [Louisville: Westminster John Knox, 1997], 84–86).

48. See further Menn, "Prayer of the Queen," 73.

49. Adele Reinhartz, "The Greek Book of Esther," in *Women's Bible Commentary*, ed. Carol A. Newsom, Sharon H. Ringe, and Jacqueline E. Lapsley, 3d ed. (Louisville: John Knox, 2012), 400.

50. Another suggestive acknowledgment of the inviolability of the Jewish people comes from within the camp of the enemy. When the plot begins to turn against Haman, his own wise men and wife declare, "If Mordecai, before whom you have begun to fall is from the seed of the Jews, you will not overcome him but will surely fall before him" (Esth. 6:13b). Note also the narrator's comment that "no one could stand before" the Jews in 9:2b.

51. See Jobes, *Esther*, 133, 138; also Grossman, *Esther*, 119, who states, "this scene comes closest to undoing God's concealment, so carefully guarded by the narrator."

52. Grossman, *Esther*, 112.

53. As Charles D. Harvey *Finding Morality in the Diaspora?: Moral Ambiguity and Transformed Morality in the Books of Esther* (Berlin: de Gruyter, 2003), 24–27 observes, however, the text does not use the standard idiom *matsa' khen* ("to find favor") but the unusual phrase *nasa' khen* ("to lift up/obtain favor"), and he may be right in suggesting that it attributes a role to Esther in earning that favor. The Septuagint Addition D greatly expands on the subtle clue to God's involvement in 5:2 by describing the wrath of the king at Esther's boldness and then narrating how "God changed the spirit of the king to gentleness" (v. 8 NETS).

54. Grossman, *Esther*, 244; Levenson, *Esther*, 18–19; Forrest S. Weiland, "Literary Clues to God's Providence in the Book of Esther," in *Bibliotheca Sacra* 160 (2003): 43–45.

55. See further Michael V. Fox, *Character and Ideology in the Book of Esther*, 2d ed. (Grand Rapids: Eerdmans, 2001), 197; Menn, "Prayer of the Queen," 78; Jobes, *Esther*, 138.

56. See Weiland, "Literary Clues," 41. Pierce "Politics of Esther and Mordecai," 84, may go too far in suggesting that Esther "desires a chance at the throne so greatly that she is willing to betray her heritage." The silence of the narrative concerning her feelings urges caution, and Pierce probably underplays the potential danger of failing to obey the king's mandate (p. 83). Esther may have complied out of fear rather than the desire for self-promotion, yet despite the risk, she was not without choice in the matter.

57. Since Mordecai expresses confidence in the Jews' deliverance, it is unclear why Esther's inaction would lead to her own destruction. His words may imply a personal threat or an assumption that God will bring judgment upon her (see further Jobes, *Esther*, 134). For an alternative reading of 4:14, see John M. Wiebe, "Esther 4:14: 'Will Relief and Deliverance Arise for the Jews from Another Place?,'" in *CBQ* 53 (1991): 409–15.

58. Grossman, *Esther*, 118.

59. Fox, *Character and Ideology*, 200.

60. Contra Mervin Breneman, *Ezra, Nehemiah, Esther*, NAC 10 (Nashville: Broadman & Holman, 1993), 336–37. See Fox who states, "This is the courage of one who must do her duty without certainty of success, without a simple faith that a higher being will protect her" (*Character and Ideology*, 200).

61. Weiland contends that the narrator of Esther "produce[d] a dramatic impression of God who was providentially superintending the affairs of His people—even when they were spiritually disinterested or ignorant of his care" ("Literary Clues," 46).

# PRAYER IN DANIEL

## WENDY L. WIDDER

## INTRODUCTION

Prayer may not be the first theme that comes to mind with respect to the book of Daniel, but it nonetheless plays an important role in the events and theology of the book. The theme of prayer arises four times in the twelve chapters. First, Daniel and his three companions in exile pray regarding Nebuchadnezzar's inscrutable dream (2:17–18), and Daniel responds to God's answered prayer with praise (2:19–23). Then, in chapter 6, Daniel's prayer routine gives Darius's officials the evidence they need to bring down Daniel (6:10–11). It is also during the early days of Darius's reign that Daniel rends his heart before Yahweh in confession of Israel's sin (chap. 9). Finally, as Daniel wrestles in chapter 10 with the revelation of a coming conflict (chap. 11–12), a divine being reports that he has come in response to Daniel's "words" before God (10:12).[1] In these four episodes, Daniel models covenant faithfulness for Diaspora Jews, and God demonstrates his loving-kindness by responding to their prayers in exile.

## THE GOD OF HEAVEN IS LORD OF ALL (DAN. 2:17–23)

In the wake of Nebuchadnezzar's fury at his experts' inability to reveal the king's dream, Daniel petitioned him (be'ah/be'e'—2:16) to give him time to do what the king demanded. Then he called his three companions together so they would seek (be'ah/be'e'—2:18) God's favor in the matter of the king's mystery and their lives would be spared. In both cases, the "seeking" of the exiles had favorable results.

The narrative gives little attention to the prayer of Daniel and his friends. It is, in fact, "twice removed" from the text: first, the prayer itself is not there, and second, the narrator does not even report that it happened. He simply reports that Daniel told his companions about the king's decree so *that* they would seek God's compassion in the matter (2:17–18). This is followed by the narrator's report that the mystery was revealed to Daniel in a night vision (2:19). From these events, the reader infers that the four men did pray and God answered.[2]

What this distance from the actual petition suggests is that the prayer itself, while the impetus for Daniel's vision, is tangential to the emphasis and focus of the text. The narrator provides enough information so we can reasonably assume what happened, but he hurries along to Daniel's response to the "God of heaven" for revealing the mystery. Here he parks for four full verses (2:20–23).

W. Sibley Towner calls Daniel's praise a "psalm of individual thanksgiving"[3] and Claus Westermann considers it a "unique development of [a declarative psalm of praise of the individual]" because the "declarative praise is introduced by descriptive praise."[4] According to this form, Daniel praised God "descriptively" for his wisdom and might, which are evidenced by his sovereign control over times, seasons, rulers, and mysteries. Then he shifts from third-person praise to first-person, in which he declares what God has done for him: namely, given him wisdom and might, and answered the Judahites' prayer.

The psalm opens with a proclamation of God's eternality, followed by a declaration that wisdom and might belong to him. The praise that follows hangs on three clause-initial words: the third-person pronoun "he" (*hu*) in 2:21 and then again in 2:22; and a lamed object preposition with a second-person singular suffix, "to you" (referring to the recipient of Daniel's praise) in 2:23.

In the first *hu'* section, Daniel details how wisdom and might belong to God (2:20). First, God controls time and seasons, and he distributes rule to humans. Second, he distributes wisdom and knowledge to humans worthy of and equipped for it. In the second *hu'* section, Daniel turns to the attributes of God that are more immediate to the matter of the king—namely, God is the one with access to deep and hidden things.

When the psalm shifts to first-person in 2:23, Daniel identifies the God of heaven—from whom the four exiles sought mercy and the one Daniel blessed (2:18–19)—as the God of his fathers. Although Daniel and his companions are far from the *land* of Israel, the *God* of Israel is still working on behalf of his people in the place of exile. Then Daniel revisits the topics of previous praise (wisdom, might, knowledge of hidden things) and acknowledges that God has given each of these things to him. He gave Daniel "wisdom and might" (2:23; cf. 2:20) and he also made known to Daniel the "matter of the king," that is, the king's dream and its interpretation. Daniel thanked God for revealing the king's mystery and for sharing his wisdom and might with Daniel (cf. 2:20–21). He received wisdom when God revealed the mystery to him, and his claim to receiving "might" anticipates his encounter with Nebuchadnezzar later in the chapter. Although God did not raise up Daniel as a king, he nonetheless used Nebuchadnezzar to bestow on Daniel significant political power (2:48).

The magnificent doxology of Daniel 2 encapsulates the primary message of the chapter—namely, wisdom and power belong to God, who gives and takes them as he pleases. This message is, in fact, a clear message of the entire book. Beginning in Daniel 1:2, where God delivered the king of Judah into the hand of the king of Babylon, God raises up kings and takes them down. He confounds the "wise" and gives wisdom and discernment to his faithful servants. He shares his wisdom, power, dominion, and even glory with humans, but he calls them to account for what they do with it. But his kingdom alone is eternal, and to him alone belong power, dominion, and glory.

Daniel's doxology affirmed for Jews under foreign rule that their God was sovereign over the nations. It also showed them the efficacy of prayer offered to their God. Finally, Daniel's recognition that the God of heaven was also the God of his fathers, reassured them that they shared in the covenantal promises of Yahweh to their ancestors.[5]

# A MODEL OF FAITHFULNESS
## (DAN. 6:10–13)

The second occurrence of prayer in the book of Daniel is in chapter 6, early in the reign of Darius. An entourage of jealous satraps conspires to entrap both Daniel and Darius so that the king will not promote the Judahite to prominence over them. The narrator details the conspiracy: no one could petition (same verb as in 2:16, 18) any god or man except Darius (6:7 [MT 6:8]). Then the narrator turns his attention to Daniel's response to the prohibition against prayer. Daniel returned home to his roof chamber with its windows opened toward Jerusalem. There he knelt, "praying and giving thanks" (6:10 [MT 6:11]). The narrator notes that this was Daniel's regular practice: three times a day, he knelt, prayed, and gave thanks at his Jerusalem-facing window. Interestingly, the narrator does not report here that Daniel actually did what was prohibited: petition God (be'ah/be'e). When the account turns to what the conspirators observed, however, they saw Daniel "petitioning and pleading" (be'e). Arguably, v. 11 (MT v. 12) reflects the point of view of the conspirators and not the narrator. [6] In other words, the satraps found what they intended to find, but the narrator presents an innocent Daniel. Later in the text Daniel also will claim his innocence (6:23).[7]

As in chapter 2, the narrator omits the content of Daniel's prayer. However, the description of Daniel's practice discloses at least two points of significance. First, the careful detailing of his routine suggests its importance both in the story and, more broadly, in Daniel's life. After the edict came down, Daniel carried on as if nothing had changed. He did what he always did, three times a day: kneel toward Jerusalem in prayer and thanks. Like his companions of chapter 3, who cast themselves at the mercy of a God who may or may not have been able to deliver them (3:17; cf. ESV and NRSV), Daniel remained faithful to the God whose house lay in ruins in Jerusalem. Under the threat of death, Daniel did not waver. His predictability gave his enemies the assurance that they would succeed in their plot, but Daniel's routine also gave Diaspora Jews an example to follow. His eventual deliverance also assured them that God does sometimes honor faithfulness by sparing life.[8]

The narrator's description of Daniel's routine is also important because it hints at the contents of the prayer. First, he says Daniel knelt, making him one of only three Old Testament characters that kneel in prayer.[9] Solomon "knelt on his knees" with outstretched hands during his great prayer of dedication (1 Kings 8:54; cf. 2 Chron. 6:13). Similarly, Ezra knelt with outstretched hands in his penitential prayer (Ezra 9:5). The similarity in posture between Solomon and Ezra, as well as the content of their prayers, connects the two accounts. The Chronicler portrays Ezra's confession of national sin as a fulfillment of Solomon's prayer of dedication. The possibility of unfaithfulness that Solomon had put before Yahweh had come to pass, and Ezra prayed that he would be merciful to his people in their confession.

The connection between Daniel's prayer and Solomon's is more tenuous since, as already noted, the narrator does not record the words of Daniel's prayer; nor does he indicate that Daniel was confessing sin.[10] The posture of kneeling in prayer, while rare in the Old Testament, may suggest a connection between Ezra and Solomon, but it is too little to take too far. However, we receive a second piece of information that provides a better reason to hear Solomon's prayer behind this episode in Daniel's life. The narrator reports that Daniel's open window, where he presumably prayed if his actions were observable, faced Jerusalem. The image of someone praying toward Jerusalem is a direct tie to Solomon's temple dedication.[11] The king repeatedly implored Yahweh to hear the prayers of his people when they prayed toward the city and the temple (1 Kings 8:29–30, 35, 38, 42, 44, 48).[12]

If Solomon's prayer is indeed the backdrop of Daniel's routine, it suggests to us what Daniel may have prayed:

> When they sin against You (for there is no man who does not sin) and You are angry with them and deliver them to an enemy, so that they take them away captive to the land of the enemy, far off or near; if they take thought in the land where they have been taken captive, and repent and make supplication to You in the land of those who have taken them captive, saying, "We have sinned and have committed iniquity, we have acted wickedly"; if they return to You with all their heart and with all their soul in the land of their enemies who have taken them captive, and pray to You toward their land which You have given to their fathers, the city which You have chosen, and the house which I have built for Your name; then hear their prayer and their supplication in heaven Your dwelling place, and maintain their cause, and forgive Your people who have sinned against You and all their transgressions which they have transgressed against You, and make them objects of compassion before those who have taken them captive, that they may

have compassion on them (for they are Your people and Your inheritance which You have brought forth from Egypt, from the midst of the iron furnace), that Your eyes may be open to the supplication of Your servant and to the supplication of Your people Israel, to listen to them whenever they call to You. (1 Kings 8:46–53 NASB)

Given this backdrop, it is interesting that the narrator does not describe Daniel's prayer as confession. Rather, Daniel was "praying and giving thanks" or "making supplication" (*metzalle' umode'*—6:10 [MT 6:11]).[13] In Solomon's prayer, the king implored Yahweh to hear the prayer and plea of his people and to maintain their cause (1 Kings 8:49). He also asked Yahweh to show the people compassion before those who took them captive (1 Kings 8:50). Since Daniel 6 does not record the specifics of Daniel's prayer, we cannot know what he prayed, but in view of 1 Kings 8:50, it may be suggestive that the rest of the chapter demonstrates the compassion of Daniel's captor (i.e., Darius) toward him.[14]

Regardless, what matters in chapter 6 is not the content of the prayer but the portrayal of Daniel as a faithful Israelite in exile, keeping the covenant and praying "without ceasing" to the God of a broken covenant. He models for Diaspora Jews what it means to be God's people, even outside the land, and he demonstrates belief that the covenant trumps the temple and the land.

## COVENANT, CONFESSION, AND A FUTURE (DAN. 9:1–23)

The third occasion of prayer in Daniel also arises early in the reign of Darius—specifically, in his first year. Daniel 9:2 finds the prophet reading the scrolls of Jeremiah, where he perceived that the desolation of Jerusalem would last seventy years. This realization, undoubtedly combined with the state of affairs "on the ground," prompted Daniel to seek the Lord in prayer and supplication, fasting in sackcloth and ashes (9:3). What follows is a long, impassioned, covenant-rich prayer in which Daniel confesses the sins of Israel and pleads for Yahweh to restore his city and his people for the sake of his name (9:4–19).

While the earlier instances of prayer in Daniel allude to the covenant (i.e., "God of my fathers" in 2:23 and the backdrop of 1 Kings 8 in Daniel 6), chapter 9 brings the covenant to center stage. It is the only place in the book where the name "Yahweh" appears, and the prayer is replete with covenant language, specifically, Deuteronomic language.[15] Mark Boda highlights such several elements:

"Lord, great and awesome God, keeping covenant and steadfast love" (9:4)

"By the hand of your servants, the prophets" (9:10)

The list of leaders (prophets, kings, princes, officials) along
with all the people of the land and the ancestors (9:6–8)

A specific confession ("we have sinned, we have done evil, we have done wrong").[16]

Gerald Wilson has made a case for the scrolls of Daniel 9:2 being letters Jeremiah sent to the exiles (Jer. 29:1–32).[17] Jeremiah had told the exilic community to settle in Babylon because they were going to be there a while—specifically, seventy years. After seventy years were "completed for Babylon," Yahweh would restore Israel (Jer. 29:10). If Daniel had access to more extensive writings of Jeremiah, he could have also been reflecting on Yahweh's promise to judge Babylon after the seventy years had been completed (see e.g. Jer. 25:12–38).

Whatever Jeremiah material Daniel was reading, he knew the time of exile should be finished: Babylon had been destroyed and the seventy years were up.[18] Wilson plausibly contends that Daniel's prayer was an attempt to meet the necessary criteria for the end of exile—namely, that Yahweh's people seek him wholeheartedly (Jer. 29:10–14; cf. Deut. 4:29–31). Ernest Lucas places the emphasis on Yahweh, not Daniel's efforts: "Daniel's prayer is intended to remind God of that prophecy and to peti-tion for mercy."[19] This focus aligns well with the thrust of Deuteronomy 4:29–31, which foresaw an exilic context: "When you are in distress and all these things have come upon you . . . you will return to Yahweh your God and you will listen to his voice. For Yahweh your God is a compas-sionate God; he will not fail you nor destroy you nor forget the covenant which he swore to your fathers."

Daniel's focus on Yahweh begins with his claim that Yahweh was his God (9:4). In chapter 2, he blessed the "God of my fathers;" in chapter 9, Daniel explicitly claims the God of his fathers, Yahweh, as his God.

Then he invokes the "Lord, the great and awesome God, who keeps the covenant and loving-kindness to those who love him and keep his commandments." Daniel prays to the God who is sovereign over the universe and has power to deliver. The book of Daniel to this point has highlighted God's sovereignty, and it has also demonstrated his power to deliver faithful servants from distress. What Daniel wants now is deliverance on a grander scale—namely, the deliverance of Yahweh's people from captivity and the restoration of Jerusalem.

More personally, Daniel is praying to the God who keeps covenant with those who love and obey him (9:4), an attribute Daniel readily admits does not belong to Israel. He then launches a series of confessions in which he admits corporate guilt. His first round of confession begins with the acknowledgement that Israel has not kept God's commands. Furthermore, when given a second chance through the prophets to obey, Israel still refused. Daniel owns the fact that Israel had willfully dug itself into a deep hole, and God was not in any way obligated to get his people out of it (vv. 5–6).

Then Daniel describes both parties of the covenant. To Yahweh belongs justice and the prerogative to judge; for the guilty Israelites, there is only deserved shame—from the greatest to the least of the people. He confesses that no one is exempt from Israel's shame. Yet, Daniel reminds Yahweh, Israel's God is merciful and forgiving—even though his people have sinned and sinned again (vv. 7–11). Daniel continues with a reflection on what Yahweh had justly done to Israel because of its unfaithfulness: he had fulfilled the covenant curses that Moses warned about. Yet, in spite of all these horrible things happening to them, Israel did not turn its face toward Yahweh. Still, "we did not listen to his voice" (9:14).

Then Daniel begins to draw his prayer to a close with a final round of confession to the God who brought his people out of Egypt and made a name for himself (vv. 15–16). Even though Israel had sinned desperately and incorrigibly, Daniel appeals to God's reputation. He had delivered Israel out of bondage once before and then threatened to destroy them (more than once) on account of their sin in the wilderness. But he relented when Moses appealed to his reputation among the nations (Exod. 32:11–14; Num. 14:13–19). Daniel pleads for forgiveness—for the sake of God's name and God's city, which had both been tarnished by his covenant partner. With a series of staccato cries, Daniel finally finishes: "Lord, listen! Lord, forgive! Lord, pay attention and act—do not delay for your sake, my God, for your name is called over your city and over your people" (9:19).

In his prayer, Daniel develops the themes of Israel's brazen sin and shame and God's greatness—that is, his power to deliver and, more importantly, his expansive mercy. Like other penitential prayers of the Persian period, Daniel 9 reflects a community experiencing God's discipline for its sin. The prophet pleads with God to bring an end to the devastation.[20]

Daniel's prayer is rich with significance. I will highlight only two things. First, by his action here on behalf of his people, Daniel stands alongside the great Old Testament prophets, the appointed faithful who identified with their people in their worst moments and interceded for them.[21] Though the book has given no hint that he is personally guilty, Daniel corporately confesses the sins of Israel. Second, to this point, the book of Daniel has been silent on the role of Israel in the occasion of the exile. The first chapter puts the people in exile, but its theological concern is to assure the people that God did it—not Nebuchadnezzar. God had not been defeated; rather, he had given his people into the hand of the Babylonian king (1:1–2). It is only now, after the book has shifted to focus on the future of Israel (beginning in Dan. 7), that we get a clear picture of the past that set the present stage. Daniel's prayer dominates the chapter because it provides the proper perspective for Diaspora Jews: Israel was rebellious, unrepentant, and deserving of its circumstances; Yahweh was gracious, forgiving, and not beholden to Israel; yet Yahweh could, with Torah precedent, reclaim his reputation, city, and sanctuary in spite of his unfaithful covenant partner. For Diaspora Jews, the great emphasis of Daniel's prayer, like that of other penitential prayers, "is on the grace of God, which provides hope that the request will be heard, and the might of God which, [sic] provides hope that the request can be fulfilled."[22] Unlike the previous occasions of prayer in Daniel, the content of Daniel's prayer *is* the focus of this chapter.

Like the unrecorded prayer in chapter 2, the prayer of Daniel 9 receives a clear answer. While Daniel is still confessing and pleading, Gabriel comes "to give him insight and understanding" as an answer to his prayer (9:21–22). It is unclear from the content of Daniel's prayer why he needed "insight and understanding," and it is also unclear how this would constitute an answer to his prayer. Daniel was praying for God to forgive the people, show his power, and restore his reputation, but the answer is Gabriel's revelation of the Seventy Weeks.[23] The immediate answer to Daniel's prayer for the end of exile turned out to be that the seventy-year exile was, indeed, about to end, but this end would be just the beginning of an even greater seventy. Grasping the connection between the two seventies, not to mention what the "greater seventy" entailed, seems to be where insight and understanding would be needed. (I discuss the Seventy Weeks further below.)

# CONFUSION AND COMFORT (DAN. 10:12)

The last occasion of prayer in the book of Daniel is an oblique reference. In the third year of Cyrus, Daniel receives an overwhelming vision that sends him into mourning and fasting during Passover and the Feast of Unleavened Bread. After three weeks, a divine being comes to Daniel and reports that Daniel's "words were heard" (10:12). Daniel had, apparently, been praying to understand the vision he had seen, and this divine being came "in response to [Daniel's] words" (10:12).

Once again the focus is not on the prayer itself. Here, the focus is on the weight of the revelation and Daniel's fervency in understanding what God had revealed. Although Daniel persisted in mourning and fasting for three weeks, the divine being assured him that his words had been heard the first day. The delay in answer was due to spiritual conflict between him, Michael, and the prince of Persia. In his words to Daniel, the divine being pulls back the curtain and gives a rare glimpse into an unseen battleground—a battleground where Daniel's prayer changed the scene.

The import of Daniel's prayer and its answer for Diaspora Jews was that God heard their prayers, even though circumstances may suggest that he hadn't. Just as chapter 1 revealed that God was in control when onlookers would have said Nebuchadnezzar's god was in control, so chapter 10 reveals that God was responsive to his people, even when they may have been tempted to think otherwise.

# A MUCKY SECOND ANSWER TO PRAYER?

A final point that may relate to the theme of prayer in Daniel is one I hesitate to raise because it requires we step into the muck of the "Dismal Swamp of OT criticism,"[24] namely, interpreting the Seventy Weeks of Daniel 9. But if one isn't willing to step in, one probably should not spend too much time in the book.

There are two references in the book of Daniel to the "first year of Darius [the Mede]," a notable textual feature in a book that is structured around dates. The first reference is in Daniel 9:1, where the narrator sets up Daniel's prayer and Gabriel's response; the second is in Daniel 11:1, where the divine being makes what appears at first blush to be a random aside. He tells Daniel that he arose in the first year of Darius to strengthen and protect Michael.[25] If this comment is not random, then perhaps the reference to the first year of Darius is a purposeful connection to Daniel 9.[26] I previously stated that the immediate answer to Daniel's prayer in chapter 9 (i.e., Gabriel's revelation of the Seventy Weeks) was a bit peculiar, given what Daniel was praying for. I suggest that Daniel 11:1 hints at a second answer to Daniel's prayer—one more directly related to his requests.

This interpretation depends on my understanding of the Seventy Weeks, which I will only detail insofar as applies to my proposal here. I assume the following:

- The "word going out to restore and rebuild Jerusalem" (9:25) refers to Jeremiah's "word" (Jer. 29:10 or 25:12), not the "decree" of a Persian king. This suggests a date of 605 or 594 BCE.[27] but since I do not interpret the numbers literally, the date is not critical.
- I split the "seven sevens" and the "sixty-two sevens" of 9:25 (reading with the MT; see also the ESV).
- The end of the seven sevens brings the first anointed one, whom I think is most likely Cyrus. [28]

Given these assumptions and the timing of the first year of Darius on the historical scene, Gabriel's words to Daniel about the coming of the anointed one after the "seven sevens" are on the verge of happening when he speaks them (9:24–27).[29] Cyrus is not officially on the scene in the book of Daniel yet, but he is about to appear and Scripture records that he will make his famous decree, resulting in the restoration and rebuilding of Jerusalem (2 Chron. 36:22–23; Ezra 1:1–2), and that is the hope for which Daniel had long prayed.[30]

Given the blurring of lines between cosmic and earthly affairs in the last half of the book, it seems plausible that Michael might have his hands full in the heavenly realms while Cyrus was contemplating or making his decree. Did anti-God angelic beings really want Israel restored to their land? Thus, Daniel's divine visitor arose to strengthen and protect Michael as he waged war on behalf of God's people in the first year of Darius, when Israel was on the cusp of being allowed to return to its land.

If this is the case, then we really have two answers to Daniel's prayer of chapter 9. The first is Gabriel in chapter 9, who expressly says he brings the answer to Daniel's prayer in the first year of Darius. The second we don't learn about until Daniel 11:1, where we discover that Daniel's visitor arose to help Michael during the first year of Darius. He does not say *why* Michael needed help, but Gabriel's message of the Seventy Weeks provides reason to think that a cosmic tumult associated with Cyrus's decree was underway. This second answer relates more directly to what Daniel asked for—namely, restoration.

# CONCLUSION

The four occasions of prayer in the book of Daniel offered Diaspora Jews confidence, encouragement, and comfort. Further, Daniel's example provided them with a model of how to live in relationship with Yahweh outside the land. In chapter two, God's prompt and life-saving answer to Daniel's prayer showed, first, that prayer to the God of Israel's fathers was still efficacious, and, second, that Israel's God was superior to all the gods of Babylon. In chapter six, Daniel's dogged faithfulness to the God of the Jerusalem temple and his subsequent deliverance from death (and the compassion of his captor) demonstrated that God honored the steadfast commitment of his followers, no matter where they were. In chapter nine, as exile dragged on and prophecies of restoration went unfulfilled, God's people could easily have questioned whether he would ever come to their aid. But Gabriel's appearance assured them that he would, and his answer gave them hope that God still had plans for his people. In chapter ten,

Daniel's distress and a delayed answer could have suggested that God was unresponsive to the needs of his people. However, the arrival of the divine being turned Daniel's eyes to a bigger world of spiritual conflict, a world in which the prayers of a faithful man could make a difference.

# DANIEL AND CHRISTIAN PRAYER

The theme of prayer in the book of Daniel offers a window into the complementary roles of God and humans in prayer, a window that is as relevant for Christians as it was for Diaspora Jews: God is sovereign and actively answering prayer; we are responsible and our prayers matter.

The sovereignty of God is a key theme throughout the book, and the instances of prayer in Daniel highlight two aspects of this sovereignty. The first is found in chapter two's declaration that wisdom and might belong to God. We pray to the God who alone is all wise and all-powerful, but this same God shares both wisdom and power with people. The apocalyptic sections of Daniel provide sobering reminders that we often will not like the people with whom God shares his power. He allows brutal and ungodly people immense power, and although he will ultimately call them to account for their abuse of such power, the suffering they cause is incomprehensible to us.

And yet, as the book of Daniel reveals, God is at work even these sufferings. When we cannot see it and it may not feel like it, God is actively working his plan—and it is a plan of cosmic consequence (Dan 10). Daniel's prayers (chap. 6 and 9) were heard and answered, though perhaps not in the way or time he wanted. God is sovereign, and we have to trust that.

Daniel exemplifies the human half of the prayer equation in his practice of prayer and in the context of this practice. He prayed perpetually (chap. 6) and persistently (chap. 10), and he prayed within the context of God's covenant (chap. 6 and 9). While the focus of Daniel's prayer was God's glory, he was keenly aware of his need to confess covenant violation and pray for mercy (chap. 9). Daniel illustrated what human faithfulness looks like: he kept the covenant—and confessed when he did not—and he prayed without ceasing according to the promises of that covenant and the character of the God who made it.

We are not under the same covenant as Daniel, but we do live in a covenant relationship with God—a covenant we are responsible to keep.

In this context of obedience, we pray in humble faith to our covenant God, trusting in his grace and mercy. We pray to the sovereign God of all wisdom and power because he is our God, and we trust that he will do what is right when it is right.

We live in a world where the news disheartens, sickens, and even leads to despair. We wonder, How long, O Lord? How long until you make all things new and right? Our experiences are not unlike those of Daniel and Diaspora Jews, and our God is the same. We pray. He hears. He answers. We may not see it, but it is so. May we be faithful in obedience and faithful in prayer

---

1. One might argue that Nebuchadnezzar prays in 4:34–35 (MT 4:31–32). However, I have excluded this text because, although Nebuchadnezzar reports that he "praised and honored God," it is unclear whether the words that follow are his prayer (note the third-person references throughout) or just his statement to "all peoples, nations, and languages" (4:1; [MT 3:31]). Daniel's praise in 2:20–23 is also in third-person, but he is clearly speaking to the God of heaven.

2. Daniel confirms this inference four verses later when he explicitly states that God made known what the men had asked of him—namely, "the matter of the king" (2:23).

3. W. Sibley Towner, *Daniel* Interpretation (Louisville: John Knox, 1984), 33.

4. Claus Westermann, *The Praise of God in the Psalms* (Richmond: Knox, 1965), 102.

5. Andrew E. Hill, *Daniel*, EBC 8 (Grand Rapids: Zondervan, 2008), 64.

6. Cf. also the conspirators' words in vv. 12–13 (MT vv. 13–14).

7. John Walton observes that Darius did not seem to foresee a problem with Daniel and the decree, and that Daniel himself claims to be innocent before the king. In his article "The Decree of Darius the Mede in Daniel 6" *JETS* 31, (1988): 279–86, he proposes a scenario in which Daniel was not technically guilty of the offense, but a weak Darius needed to bow to the demands of his officials. I like Walton's proposal, though he admits his hypothesis is tenuous given a relative lack of evidence, but the narrative also seems to highlight Daniel's unwavering faithfulness to God in the face of imminent danger. Verse 10 (MT vs. 11) gives the impression that Daniel knew where his actions would lead.

8. The words of Shadrach, Meshach, and Abednego as they faced death (3:17–18) caution against promising God's deliverance from trials. However, there remains the promise of his ultimate deliverance (12:1–3), a hope that would have resonated with Daniel's Diaspora audience.

9. The only other Old Testament reference to kneeling before God is Psalm 95:6, which seems to describe a posture of worship, not specifically a posture of prayer.

10. However, Solomon asked Yahweh to hear his people's prayers when they made supplication (Hithpael of *khnn*; see, e.g., 1 Kings 8:47, 49). The conspirators observe Daniel making supplication (Aramaic Hithpael of *khnn*; Dan 6:11 [MT 6:12]), though my case would be stronger here if the narrator's report in 6:10 (MT 6:11) said this instead of "praying and giving thanks" (*metzalle' umode'*).

11. Jordan M. Scheetz sees the mention of the holy city here as part of the book's "focus on Jerusalem" that begins in the first verse when Nebuchadnezzar besieges the city (cf. 1:1–2, 5:2–4; 9:2, 16, 18–19), but he does not suggest any further significance of its presence in

Dan 6 (*The Concept of Canonical Intertextuality and the Book of Daniel* [Eugene: Pickwick, 2011], 108–9).

12. Cf. 2 Chron. 6:20–21, 26, 29, 34, 38.

13. The tnk and James Montgomery both translate *mode'* as "confessing," not "thanking." In his translation, Montgomery notes Dan. 9:4, where Daniel is clearly said to be confessing (*va'ethvaddeh*), so it appears that his translation of *mode'* as "confessing" has been influenced by Dan. 9:4 (James A. Montgomery, *A Critical and Exegetical Commentary on the Book of Daniel*, in ICC [New York: Charles Scribner's Sons, 1927], 274).

14. Greg Goswell discusses as well the relationship between Daniel's prayer in chapter six and in chapter nine and suggests that the prayer of chapter 9 gives us the content of Daniel's regular prayer in chapter six. See "The Temple Theme in the Book of Daniel, *JETS* 55.3 (2012), 512–14.

15. Towner concludes that more than 85 percent of the prayer is quotations (*Daniel*, 129). Montgomery details where similar language is found, but says that Daniel's prayer is not "slavishly dependent upon" the other texts (*Daniel*, 361–68).

16. Mark J. Boda, *Praying the Tradition: The Origin and Use of Tradition in Nehemiah 9* BZAW 277 (Berlin: Walter de Gruyter, 1999), 43–50. Boda and others have dealt extensively with the content of Daniel's prayer and with its relationship to other texts. See also M. J. Boda, "The Priceless Gain of Penitence: From Communal Lament to Penitential Prayer in the 'Exilic' Liturgy of Israel," *Horizons in Biblical Theology* 25 (2003): 51–75; and Jordan M. Scheetz, *The Concept of Canonical Intertextuality and the Book of Daniel* (Eugene: Pickwick, 2011), esp. 129–46.

17. Gerald H. Wilson, "The Prayer of Daniel 9: Reflection on Jeremiah 29," *JSOT* 48 (1990): 91–99.

18. I do not consider seventy to be the literal number of years "required" for the exile. Its use elsewhere in the Bible with respect to the time of exile (see, esp., 2 Chron. 36:21) and in other contexts (e.g., Gen. 46:27; Deut. 10:22; Ps. 90:10) indicates that it is often a symbolic number, representing a human lifespan or completeness.

19. Ernest C. Lucas, *Daniel*, in AOTC 20, eds. David W. Baker and Gordon J. Wenham (Downers Grove, IL: InterVarsity Press, 2002), 236.

20. Boda, "The Priceless Gain of Penitence," 52–53. See also Ezra 9; Neh. 1, 9; cf. Ps. 106.

21. For example, Moses (Exod. 32–33), Samuel (1 Sam. 12), and Jeremiah (Jer. 4:13–26).

22. Ibid., 55.

23. See also Moses in Exod. 32–33 and Num. 14.

24. Montgomery, *Daniel*, 400.

25. The text is ambiguous about whether Daniel's divine visitor arose to help Michael or Darius. Commentators are divided on the issue, but my proposal does not depend on the referent. I assume it is Michael, but if it is Darius, the blurred lines between earthly and spiritual conflict in the second half of Daniel allow us to blur the lines between Michael and an earthly king favorably disposed to God's people.

26. Many commentators note that 11:1 identifies the ministering being of chapter 10 as Gabriel (see, e.g. Lucas, *Daniel*, 278). I do not consider this divine being to be Gabriel but rather a theophany.

27. Holladay dates Jeremiah 29 to 594 BCE, based on its presence after chapters 27–28 and its assumption of "optimistic prophets in Babylon," a placement and tone that suggest a relationship to the attempted revolt against Nebuchadnezzar in December 595/January 594. See William L. Holladay, *Jeremiah 2*, Hermeneia (Minneapolis: Fortress, 1989), 140.

28. Some form and assortment of these assumptions belong to at least two different interpretations of the Seventy Weeks: the Antiochene (or Maccabean) Approach and a symbolic eschatological view. See John H. Walton, "Views Concerning Daniel's 70 Weeks" in *Chronological and Background Charts of the Old Testament* (Grand Rapids: Zondervan, 1994), 106. See also Thomas E. McComiskey, "The Seventy 'Weeks' of Daniel against the Background of Ancient Near Eastern Literature," *WTJ* 47 (1985): 18–45. These views differ in their interpretations beyond the point of Cyrus, the first anointed one.

29. Regardless of the identity of the mysterious Darius, his first year coincides with the end of the Babylon Empire (Dan. 5:30–31).

30. Cyrus is, of course, mentioned in Daniel 1:21, and again in 6:28. He may also be the same person as Darius the Mede. But, strictly speaking, he is not part of the narrative framework until 10:1, when Daniel receives a vision in the Cyrus's third year.

# Prayer in 1–2 Chronicles, Ezra, and Nehemiah

## Claude Mariottini

## The Scope of the Project

The purpose of this chapter is to study the theology of prayer in Chronicles, Ezra, and Nehemiah. Until recently, it was the scholarly consensus that 1–2 Chronicles and Ezra–Nehemiah were two components of a single work known as the Chronicler's History, a work that covers Israel's history from Adam to the time of Nehemiah. However, recent scholarship has concluded that the book of Chronicles is a separate work from Ezra–Nehemiah. Although the date for the composition of these books is debated, Chronicles is probably the work of an author who was different from the author of Ezra-Nehemiah.

These three books will be treated together in this study because they share a similar theological outlook. These books were written at a time when the temple and the priesthood were the focus of the *golah* community. The temple was the focus of the community because it was the place where God lived and the place where the community should come and worship. In the days of Ezra and Nehemiah this community was threatened with losing its distinctive character as a holy people.[1] The people undergirded their work of building the walls of Jerusalem and making religious reforms with prayers to God.

# PRAYERS IN THE BOOK OF CHRONICLES

The prayers that are recorded in Chronicles came out of the intensive personal relationship the people had with God and out of the trust and confidence they had that God "was attentive" to their prayers (2 Chr. 7:15).[2] This confidence grew out of the worship and praise of God that took place in the temple. In the theology of the Chronicler, the worship of God included not only sacrifices but also praise, prayer, and music. Although the people of Israel knew that it was not necessary to pray only at a sacred place in Jerusalem, they were aware that the full expression of worship was a communal celebration that took place at special occasions in the religious life of Israel. There are two items that distinguish the Chronicler as a theologian: his view of the temple and his emphasis on prayer.

## Chronicles and the Temple

The temple played an important role in the theology of the Chronicler for it served as a constant reminder that Israel was the people of God. The Chronicler used many different designations to describe the temple in Jerusalem. The Chronicler said that the temple was an exalted house (2 Chron. 6:2), a place where Yahweh would live forever (2 Chron. 6:2). The temple was God's dwelling place (2 Chron. 6:21).

The temple was a house of prayer for all people (2 Chron. 6:32–33; cf. Isa 56:7), a place where God would be accessible to everyone who called on him in time of need. Of the temple, God said: "My eyes and my heart will be there for all time" (2 Chron. 7:16). Since God's heart was in the temple, anyone who prayed to him was assured that God was attentive to their prayers, even when they prayed from "the land of their captivity" (2 Chron. 6:38). To the Chronicler, the natural setting for prayer was the temple, the place Yahweh had chosen to reveal his name. Communal prayers and prayers in times of emergencies were prayed in the temple, although the Bible clearly shows that prayers could be uttered anywhere by a person in need of God's favor.

## Prayers in Chronicles

The prayers found in the book of Chronicles reflect the theological concerns of the Chronicler.[3] Several of the prayers that appear in 1–2

Chronicles do not appear in the sources the Chronicler used in the preparation of his work. There are twenty-three references to prayers or to people praying in Chronicles. Nine times the Chronicler says that people prayed, but he does not provide the words of their petitions to God. Fourteen times the Chronicler says that people are praying and he then gives the words of their prayers. Thirteen prayers are unique to the Chronicler, nine prayers in Chronicles either appear in or are adapted from Samuel and Kings, and one prayer is taken from the book of Psalms. The prayers in Chronicles are classified as follows: There are two prayers in the genealogies, eighteen royal prayers, two Levitical prayers, and one prayer by the warriors of Abijah. The royal prayers are divided as follows: There are six prayers of David, three by Solomon, one by Asa, three by Jehoshaphat, four by Hezekiah, and one by Manasseh.

The Chronicler used several different words to refer to prayer and the way people approached God. The Chronicler used the following words to refer to the way people came before God to ask for divine help:

1. The verb *qara'* means "to call" but when used in the context of prayer, it carries the idea of appealing to God and it is translated "call" (1 Chron. 16:8), "invoke" (2 Chron. 6:33).

2. The verb *'amar* is generally translated "to say," "to speak." When used in the context of prayer, the word refers to a person speaking to God in prayer (1 Chron. 21:17).

3. The verb *sha'al* means "to ask," "to inquire." When the word is used in the context of prayer, the word means to make a specific request of God (1 Chron. 4:10).

4. The verb *za'aq* means "to cry." When used in the context of prayer, the verb means "to call for help," "to cry out," "to cry for help" (1 Chron. 5:20).

5. The verb *tsa'aq* means "to cry," "to cry for help." The verb appears only once in Chronicles (2 Chron. 13:14) with the meaning "to cry for help." In the context of prayer, the verb expresses a prayer of distress.

6. The verb *'atar* means "to pray," "to entreat" (1 Chron. 5:20).

7. The verb *darash* means "to seek guidance," "to inquire." In the book of Chronicles, the expression "to seek," *darash*, appears thirty-seven times. When the word is used in the context of prayer, it generally has the idea of seeking God for guidance (e.g., 1 Chron. 10:14).[4]

8. The verb *khanan* means "to be gracious," "to show favor." When the word is used in the context of prayer, the verb means "to seek favor," "to plead," "to make supplication" (2 Chron. 6:24).

9. The word *palal* occurs fifteen times in 1–2 Chronicles. The verb *palal* means to "pray" (e.g., 2 Chron. 30:18) and the noun *tefilah* occurs twelve times and it means "prayer" (e.g., 2 Chron. 7:15).

10. The noun *rinnah* carries the idea of raising one's voice in the sense of rejoicing. When the word is used in the context of prayer, it means, "a cry," "lamentation," "a supplication for favor" (2 Chron. 6:19).

11. The verb *khalah* means "to be sick," "to be weak." In the context of prayer, the word is used of Manasseh entreating the favor of Yahweh (2 Chron. 33:12).

12. The verb *zakhar* means "to remember," "to invoke." Although the word does not appear in the context of prayer, the Chronicler says that David appointed "certain of the Levites as ministers before the ark of the LORD, to invoke, to thank, and to praise the LORD, the God of Israel" (1 Chron. 16:4).

## Postures in Prayer

As for the posture in prayer, Solomon's actions during the prayer of dedication of the temple reveal some of the postures of the people as they prayed to God. The text in Chronicles mentions standing and kneeling (2 Chron. 6:13). This probably indicates that during his prayer, Solomon changed his posture as he prayed before the Lord. First, he stood to praise the Lord and then knelt to confess the nation's sin and to entreat the favor of the Lord on behalf of the people.[5]

Solomon spread his hands toward heaven, the place that was considered to be God's dwelling place (2 Chron. 6:33, 39). Since the temple would become Yahweh's new dwelling place on earth, it was also possible that Solomon was raising his hand toward the new temple (cf. 1 Kings 8:38). This probably became the attitude of those in exile as demonstrated by Daniel who prayed three times a day with the windows of his chamber opened toward Jerusalem (Dan. 6:10).

Other attitudes and postures of prayer are found in Chronicles. David sat before the Lord and prayed (1 Chron. 17:16). This position of prayer refers to squatting before God. At the dedication of the temple, the people "bowed down on the pavement with their faces to the ground" (2 Chron. 7:3). During a time of fasting, Jehoshaphat led the people in prayer (2 Chron. 20:3–12). In the worship of God in the temple, the Chronicler mentions music by the congregation, singers, musical instruments, praising God, offering thanksgiving, and prayers of petition, thanksgiving, intercession, and lament.

# THE THEOLOGY OF PRAYER IN CHRONICLES

In his article on prayers in Chronicles, Pancratius C. Beentjes states that the prayers in the book of Chronicles "are best understood as a condensing of the Chronicler's most important theological notions."[6] The theological ideology of the Chronicler is found in his use of the material taken from Samuel and Kings. When using his sources, the Chronicler at times used the same words of the prayers found in Samuel and Kings. However, at times he changed his sources in order to present his theological perspective. One example is found in Solomon's prayer at the dedication of the temple, where the Chronicler changed Solomon's prayer in 1 Kings 8:22–53 and removed a section of the prayer (verses 51–53) and added a section from Psalm 132:8–10 into his version of the prayer (2 Chron. 6:40–42).[7]

The reason for the change is based on the fact that the Chronicler was appealing to God to remember his steadfast love for David (2 Chron. 6:42) instead of Solomon's original appeal to the redemption of Israel from the iron furnace of Egypt (1 Kings 8:51). He was also reinterpreting the religious traditions of the past to reflect the religious needs of the post-exilic community of his days.

In the theology of the Chronicler, those kings who sought Yahweh, Asa (2 Chron. 14:7 [MT 14:6]), Jehoshaphat (2 Chron. 20:3), Uzziah (2 Chron. 26:5), and Hezekiah (2 Chron. 31:21), were the ones who were considered to be faithful, who promoted the reforms of the temple, and the ones who prevailed in battle. The theology of the Chronicler also appears in the prayers of Asa, Jehoshaphat, and Hezekiah. These kings are presented as models of piety and faithfulness for the community of the Chronicler's day and their prayers became models of cultic faithfulness.

## The Chronicler and Prayer

The book of Chronicles is addressed to the restored community of Judah who lived under Persian domination in the fourth century BCE. The Chronicler is concerned above all with the restoration of the community and the means by which God would bless the people.

To the Chronicler, the hope of restoration lays with the worship of God in the temple and the community's participation in the religious life of the nation. The community would eventually face many difficult times and experience the horrors of drought, locust, and pestilence. When the people faced those circumstances, the means by which they would find divine forgiveness and restoration would be through repentance and prayer.

> If my people who are called by my name humble themselves,
> pray, seek my face, and turn from their wicked ways, then I will
> hear from heaven, and will forgive their sin and heal their land.
> (2 Chron. 7:14)

The Chronicler believed that God was attentive to the people's prayer and in his work he provided several instances of God answering the prayers of those who sought him, who humbled themselves, and prayed. But the Chronicler, writing at a time when the monarchy no longer existed, placed the burden of prayer on the people: "If my people . . . pray." If the people prayed, Yahweh would forgive them. If the people prayed, Yahweh would heal them.

The Chronicler believed in the power of prayer and he believed that there would be healing and forgiveness when the people came to God's house to worship him and participate in the religious life of the community. To the Chronicler, God's presence in the temple "highlights God's continuing commitment to Israel and the central role played by the temple as a house of prayer and [as] a symbol of God's eternal will to forgive."[8]

# Prayers in the Book of Ezra

Prayers in the book of Ezra are not as numerous as in the book of Chronicles. There is only one prayer in Ezra in which the words of the prayer are given in full, the penitential prayer in Ezra 9:6–15. There are three other references to prayers in the book: Ezra 6:10, 8:23, and 10:1.

## Praying for the King: Ezra 6:10

The reference to prayer in Ezra 6:10 is a request of Darius, king of Persia, which he made at the time a decree was written authorizing Ezra to return to Jerusalem to rebuild the temple. In his decree Darius made provisions for the rebuilding of the temple by providing from the royal treasury all that was needed for the project so that the priests in the new temple could "offer pleasing sacrifices to the God of heaven, and pray for the life of the king and his children" (Ezra 6:10).

## Supplication for a Safe Journey: Ezra 8:21–23

As Ezra prepared to return to Jerusalem, he proclaimed a fast and invited the people with him to seek God and pray for a safe journey.[9] In this text, two words for prayers are used, but the NRSV used three different words to translate them. The verb *baqash* appears in verses 21 and 23. The basic meaning of the word is "to seek." When the word is used in the context of seeking God, the word acquires the meaning of prayer.[10] In verse 21 the NRSV translates the word as "to seek" and in verse 23 as "petitioned." The second word is *'atar*, a word that means "to pray" or "to supplicate." According to BDB, this supplication is always addressed to God.[11] The NRSV translates the word *'atar* as "entreaty."

This prayer by Ezra and the people traveling with him to Jerusalem reveals the people's belief that prayers to God had a beneficial outcome.

Ezra and the people were afraid of the perils of traveling with family and transporting goods on a long journey. Thus, they fasted and prayed and entrusted their safety to God. Ezra was confident that God was gracious to "all who seek him" (v. 22). As a result of their faith and the power of prayer, they traveled to Jerusalem and arrived there safely. Their safe trip was evidence to Ezra that God had listened to their prayer and given them a safe trip.

## Ezra's Penitential Prayer: Ezra 9:6–15

The penitential prayer of Ezra occurred as a reaction to the news that the men of the *golah* community had married foreign women and were making arrangements for their sons also to marry foreign women. Ezra was joined by a group of faithful people, "all who trembled at the words of the God of Israel" (Ezra 9:4; 10:3), in confessing and praying for the sins of the nation.

After Ezra heard about the problem, he tore his garments. He also plucked off the hair of his head and of his beard, and sat down before the house of God appalled, deeply shocked by the situation. Ezra remained in mourning and in prayer until the time of the evening sacrifice. Ezra then says, "And at the evening sacrifice I rose from my fasting, with my garments and my mantle rent, and fell upon my knees and spread out my hands to the LORD my God" (9:5).

Ezra's prayer is typical of the penitential prayers of the post-exilic community. However, in contrast to the penitential prayers in Nehemiah 1 and 9 and Daniel 9, Ezra's prayer is not a prayer of petition. He does not ask anything from God. Ezra's prayer does not have a request for forgiveness. In his prayer Ezra speaks of the apostasy of past generations and claims divine mercy in order to stop another judgment that will come if the nation does not repent.

His prayer is addressed to the God of Israel. The prayer contains three appeals to God: "My God," "Our God," and "Yahweh, God of Israel." Yahweh, the sacred name of God, appears twice in Ezra's prayer (9:8, 15). Twice Ezra used first person language "My God" (9:6 [2x]) to make his appeal to God. Six times Ezra uses "our God" in his prayer to declare the sins of the people before God (9:8[2x], 9 [2x], 10, 13). Ezra's prayer, then, is a communal prayer. He uses the plural "our" twenty times as he prays to God on behalf of the people. In his prayer, Ezra confesses the guilt of the people. Four times he uses the word "guilt" to acknowledge their iniquity before God (9:6, 7, 13, 15).

Ezra recognizes that it was because of God's mercy that a remnant had survived. Four times Ezra mentions the remnant in his prayer (9:8, 13, 14, 15). The survival of a remnant of Israel and their return back to their land is evidence of God's grace and mercy toward his people. In his confession of sins, three times Ezra refers to God's grace as the reason for the survival of Israel (9:8–9, 13, 15). The Hebrew word *tekhinnah*, which is translated as "favor" in 9:8, appears in Solomon's prayer of the dedication of the temple as "supplication" (2 Chron. 6:29), a prayer made by the people asking for God's help and mercy in times of need.

## The Response to Ezra's Prayer: Ezra 10:1

The reference to prayer in Ezra 10:1 describes the manner in which Ezra prayed the penitential prayer of 9:6–15 and describes what happened while Ezra was praying. The text says that, in his prayer, Ezra made confession in which he mentioned the sins of the people and their rebellion against God. During his prayer, Ezra was weeping and prostrated on the ground before the house of God. As a result of Ezra's loud crying, a large crowd composed of men, women, and children gathered around him and they also wept bitterly. Ezra's prayer moved the people to express their remorse publicly and join Ezra in repenting of their sins.

After Ezra prayed and interceded for the community, he left from the place where he prayed in front of the temple and went to a special room belonging to Jehohanan. While there, Ezra did not eat food or drink water because he was mourning for the sins of the people. Though fasting is usually accompanied by prayer (2 Chron. 20:3–4), the text does not mention any prayer made by Ezra on this occasion.

"Made confession" (10:1) translates the Hitpael of *yadah*, which, according to Alexander, "is normally employed when this verb is used to convey the confession of national sins."[12] This verb appears in the great national confessions found in Nehemiah 1:6; 9:2–3, and Daniel 9:4, 20. As a result of Ezra's prayer, the people were moved by Ezra's words and humbled themselves before the Lord. They confessed their sins and made a covenant with God in which they promised under oath to live by the demands of the covenant and send away the foreign women.

# PRAYERS IN THE
# BOOK OF NEHEMIAH

A quick review of the prayers in the book of Nehemiah reveals that Nehemiah was a man who believed in the power of prayer. Many of his prayers came out of the problems he faced in rebuilding the walls of Jerusalem. Nehemiah prayed because he recognized he needed divine guidance and help to accomplish his work. These prayers reflect Nehemiah's personal relationship with God and reveal that he believed God was a God who answers prayers.

Nehemiah's prayers teach important aspects about the character of God. To him, God was working in the history of his people and in the affairs of nations. Nehemiah prayed often. He prayed to God in different ways, at different times, and in all circumstances. There are twelve prayers in the book of Nehemiah.

## Nehemiah's Penitential Prayer: Nehemiah 1:4–11

Nehemiah's prayer comes out of the context of the difficult situation facing the Jewish community in Jerusalem. When Nehemiah heard that the wall and the gates of Jerusalem were broken and the great shame the residents of the city were facing, he became greatly distressed.

Nehemiah was a pious man. He took time to grieve for the condition of the city and for the situation of the people of Judah. He sat down on the ground, a customary posture in mourning and fasting. Weeping and mourning are common responses to grief. He then fasted. Fasting and praying reflects post-exilic piety (Ezra 9:3–5).[13] People also fasted before asking for divine favors, before embarking on a great undertaking, or when facing danger. Nehemiah was fasting and praying for the condition of the people in Jerusalem and for himself, seeking divine guidance and help on how to deal with the helpless situation of the people. Before Nehemiah approached the king of Persia to ask for help, he turned to God in prayer for guidance.

The structure of Nehemiah's prayer is similar to the penitential prayers of Ezra and Daniel. The prayer begins with an address to God, followed by an appeal to God to hear his prayer and a confession of sins. Nehemiah asks God to remember the promise he made to Moses. He then ends his prayer with an intercession for the people and a personal request for success in his dealing with the king.

Nehemiah confesses the sins of the nation. Throughout the history of Israel God had been faithful to the special relationship he established with the people through the covenant. God promised to bless the people if they were faithful in keeping the obligations to which they were bound by the covenant. In his prayer, Nehemiah emphasized that the people were not faithful to the promises they had made to God. Nehemiah said that the people had sinned against God because of their unfaithfulness: "We have offended you deeply" (Neh. 1:7). He identifies himself with the sinful people by saying, "I and my family have sinned" (Neh. 1:6).

Before he went to see Artaxerxes and request permission to go to Jerusalem to help the people, Nehemiah prayed. He was uncertain whether the king would grant him permission to travel to Jerusalem. Thus, he sought divine help before approaching the Persian king. His prayer shows his faith and trust in God and his awareness that God was involved in the affairs of nations.

## Prayer for Guidance, Nehemiah 2:4

Nehemiah's prayer in 2:4 occurred three months after his previous prayer.[14] He waited for an ideal time to approach the king. While Nehemiah was carrying out his duties, the king realized that something was bothering him. When asked the reason for his sadness, Nehemiah told the king about the desperate condition of Jerusalem and how the city lay in ruins. The king asked Nehemiah, "What do you request?" Before Nehemiah presented his petition to the king, he paused for a brief silent prayer: "So I prayed to the God of heaven" (Neh. 2:4).

Although the words of the prayer are not given, Nehemiah's brief prayer shows that he had incorporated the habit of prayer into every aspect of his life. He was about to request of the king of Persia permission to go to Jerusalem, but he decided to ask God for guidance in what to say so that God would move the king into allowing him to travel to Jerusalem. Nehemiah's prayer was not a frantic call for help. Rather, he was placing the outcome of his request in the hands of God. Nehemiah wanted to ensure that God would guide the decision of the king. His declaration that he received everything he asked (2:8) is an affirmation that God had answered his prayer.

## Prayer for Vindication: Nehemiah 4:4–5 [MT 3:36–37]

This prayer for vindication arises out of the resistance Nehemiah encountered from those who opposed the rebuilding of the wall. After Nehemiah started rebuilding the wall, several local officials openly opposed the project by scorning and mocking the workers (4:1-3 [MT 3:33–35]). Nehemiah took a strong stance against his detractors because they were opposing the work of God.

Nehemiah asks God to remember what his opponents are saying about the workers. In his cry to God, he asks for justice. He wants the words of their detractors to be turned back on them and that which they wished for the workers would happen upon their own heads. Nehemiah's prayer of vindication asks God that the enemies of the people be scorned and mocked, that their sins may not be forgiven, and that they become booty of war in the hands of their enemies.

Nehemiah's prayers reflect the sentiment of the psalmist when he prayed and asked God to allow the children of the Babylonians to be dashed against the rocks (Ps 137:9). Although Nehemiah's language may be offensive to modern sensibilities, his prayer must be understood in the context of the post-exilic community. Nehemiah believed his detractors were opposing God's work.[15] His prayer is not a prayer for vengeance, but a prayer for vindication and for divine justice. Rather than using his power, granted to him by the Persian king, Nehemiah called upon God to vindicate his work and bring judgment against those who opposed God.

## Prayer for Protection, Nehemiah 4:9 [MT 4:3]

After Nehemiah prayed for vindication against his enemies, the work of rebuilding the wall continued with success. When the enemies saw that the work was progressing and that the gaps were being closed, they became very angry and made plans to disrupt the work. Nehemiah and the community came together to pray and ask God for help. At the same time Nehemiah set guards to protect the wall and the workers against those who threaten them. He interpreted the lack of action by his enemies as a divine response to his prayer for he knew that "God had frustrated their plan" (Neh. 4:15 [MT 4:9]).

## Prayer for Strength: Nehemiah 6:9

This brief prayer arises as Nehemiah continues to face the opposition of his enemies. After the repair of the wall was finished, Nehemiah's enemies developed a scheme to harm him. They falsely accused Nehemiah of planning to rebel against Persian authority. They also tried to frighten the workers so that they would stop their work. Confronted with this situation, Nehemiah prays: "But now, O God, strengthen my hands" (Neh. 6:9).

Scholars are divided on whether 6:9 is a prayer to God. The vocative "O God" is not in the Hebrew text. The NIV translates the verse as a personal prayer of Nehemiah, "But I prayed, 'Now strengthen my hands,'" even though the words "I prayed" are not in the Hebrew text. Both Fensham and Blenkinsopp do not believe Nehemiah's words constitute a prayer. Both Miller[16] and Balentine[17] believe this is a short prayer by Nehemiah. In my opinion, 6:9 is a short prayer that reflects Nehemiah's concern over the threat posed by his enemies.

## The Levitical Prayer: Nehemiah 9:5–37

This liturgical prayer presents a survey of Israel's history, a confession of sin, and a petition requesting deliverance from the people's oppressive situation. Scholars differ on who prayed this prayer. The NRSV, following the Septuagint, adds to 9:6 "And Ezra said," an expression that is lacking in the Hebrew text. Most translations attribute this prayer to the Levites and not to Ezra. In Nehemiah 9:4–5, the Levites are leading the liturgy and praying with a loud voice to God. Thus, the prayer begins in 9:5 with the Levitical call to worship and not with 9:6, as suggested by the change proposed by the Septuagint and followed by the NRSV.

According to Newman, the Levitical prayer of Nehemiah 9:5-37 is a good example of Second Temple era prayers that reflect the use of scripture to present a historical retrospect of what God has done in the history of Israel.[18] The purpose of the prayer is to address the present situation of the community. The prayer refers to God's gracious and merciful dealings with Israel in the past in order to ask for divine help in the present. The appeal to the character of God in Exodus 34:6–7 is an appeal to God's dealing with Israel. These characteristics of God are linked with God's continued commitment to Israel and his forgiving love. God is called the God who keeps covenant and steadfast love (Neh. 9:32), an expression which also appears in Nehemiah 1:5 and Daniel 9:4. This may indicate that the phrase was part of the liturgical language of the post-exilic community.[19] The use of *khesed* in Nehemiah 9:32 emphasizes the special relationship that existed between Yahweh and Israel because of the covenant. The word *khesed* expresses God's faithful love for Israel.

The divine attributes listed in Exodus 34:6-7 appear five times in this Levitical prayer. By reciting important events and periods in the history of Israel, the Levites are emphasizing that throughout its history the people sinned against God and their rebellion led to the great distress they were facing in the present.

The prayer emphasizes the transcendence of God. He is called great, mighty, and awesome. The prayer also emphasizes the special relationship that existed between God and Israel. God was faithful to the promises he had made to Israel. Twice God is called *tsaddiq*, just or righteous (9:8, 33). This word is used in the prayer to declare that the judgment Yahweh brought upon Israel was deserved because Israel had disobeyed the commandments that resulted in the people becoming servants of the Persian government.

The theological emphasis of this prayer is found in what it says about God and Israel. The prayer affirms that Yahweh is a gracious and merciful God who is faithful to keep the covenant and who loves his people with an abiding love. Throughout its history, Israel had been unfaithful to God by sinning against his will and by not keeping the demands of the covenant. The nation deserved the punishment it received, but confronted with their oppressive situation, in their distress, the people threw themselves on the mercy and compassion of God, hoping once again for deliverance from their oppressive condition.

## The "Remember Me" "Remember Them" Prayers

In the book of Nehemiah there are several prayers in which Nehemiah asks God to remember. Four prayers ask God to remember him for the things he has done (Neh. 5:19; 13:14, 13:22; 13:31). Two prayers ask God to remember his enemies for what they have done (Neh. 6:14; 13:29). These personal prayers of Nehemiah have elicited different views by scholars. For instance, Blenkinsopp believes that these prayers "should be viewed as symptomatic of a venal and legalistic religious attitude."[20] Kidner believes that these prayers spring from Nehemiah's love and "tireless zeal" for God.[21] In his studies of these prayers, Holmgren says they must be understood in the context of the covenant between God and Israel.[22] Because of the relationship established by the covenant, God pleads with Israel to remember the good things he has done for them. However, this relationship is reciprocal. God has a responsibility to remember Israel in her hour of need (Exod. 2:24). The people of Israel expected God to keep his commitment to Israel. This conviction that God honors his covenant with Israel is behind all of Nehemiah's prayer: "O LORD God of heaven, the great and awesome God who keeps covenant and steadfast love with those who love him and keep his commandments" (Neh. 1:5).

Nehemiah's prayers reveal the heart of a pious individual, a man of faith, commitment, and conviction. His life of prayer arises out of his conviction that he was doing God's will. His prayers provide insight into God's character. Nehemiah believed that God honored his covenant with Israel because he was a loving and merciful God, faithful, trustworthy and just in his relationship with his people.

# CONCLUSION

In seeking to formulate a theology of prayer in the books of Chronicles, Ezra, and Nehemiah we conclude that there is not *a* theology of prayer in these books but many. We also discover that there is not one way to pray but many. The prayers in the books of Chronicles, Ezra, and Nehemiah are post-exilic prayers. They are prayers that reflect a rich tradition of prayers in Israel. These post-exilic prayers have a different style from prayers in the Pentateuch and in the prophets. These prayers have different concerns. Post-exilic prayers are primarily prayers of confession, although intercession, petition, thanksgiving, and praise are also found in the books of Chronicles, Ezra, and Nehemiah.

The people of Israel prayed to the Lord their God because they believed he would answer their prayers: "O you who answer prayer! To you all flesh shall come" (Ps 65:2). They prayed because they knew God was a compassionate God who forgave and blessed. Like Israel, God's people today pray because God is still gracious and merciful, a God who hears the prayers of those who call unto him.

1. On the *golah* community, see Rainer Kessler, *The Social History of Ancient Israel* (Minneapolis: Fortress Press, 2008), 128-157.

2. All references will be taken from the *New Revised Standard Version* (NRSV) unless otherwise indicated.

3. On prayers in Chronicles, see Pancratius C. Beentjes, "Psalms and Prayers in the Book of Chronicles," *Psalms and Prayers*, in OTS 55, eds. Bob Becking and Eric Peels (Leiden: Brill, 2007), 9–44 and Samuel E. Balentine, "'You Can't Pray a Lie': Truth *and* Fiction in the Prayers of Chronicles," *The Chronicler as Historian* (Sheffield: Sheffield Academic Press, 1997), 255.

4. On the use of *darash* in the book of Chronicles, see Christopher C. Begg, "'Seeking Yahweh' and the Purpose of Chronicles," in *LS* 9 (1982): 128–141.

5. D. R. Ap-Thomas, "Notes on Some Terms Relating to Prayer," *VT* 6 (1956): 226.

6. Pancratius C. Beentjes, "Psalms and Prayers in the Book of Chronicles," *Psalms and Prayers*, OTS 55 (Leiden: Brill, 2007), 9.

7. See the discussion in Mark Throntveit, *When Kings Speak: Royal Speeches and Prayers in Chronicles*, SBLDS 93 (Atlanta: Scholars Press, 1987), 60–61.

8. Martin J. Selman, *1 Chronicles*, TOTC (Downers Grove: InterVarsity, 1994), 44.

9. Joseph Blenkinsopp, *Ezra-Nehemiah*, OTL (Philadelphia: Westminster, 1988), 168, says that fasting "often acts as a reinforcement of prayer."

10. O. R. Sellers, "Seeking God in the Old Testament," *JBR* 21 (1953): 234–37.

11. BDB, 801.

12. *TWOT*, 1:845.

13. Blenkinsopp, *Ezra–Nehemiah*, 207.

14. Ibid., 213.

15. Mervin Breneman, *Ezra, Nehemiah, Esther*, NAC (Nashville: Broadman & Holman, 1993), 194–95.

16. Patrick D. Miller, *They Cried to the Lord: The Form and Theology of Biblical Prayer* (Minneapolis: Fortress, 1994), 94.

17. Samuel E. Balentine, *Prayer in the Hebrew Bible: The Drama of Divine-Human Dialogue* (Minneapolis: Fortress, 1993), 19.

18. Judith H. Newman, *Praying by the Book: The Scripturalization of Prayer in Second Temple Judaism* (Atlanta: Scholars Press, 1999), 56.

19. Ibid., 102.

20. Blenkinsopp, *Ezra-Nehemiah*, 265.

21. Derek Kidner, *Ezra and Nehemiah*, TOTC, ed. Donald J. Wiseman (Downers Grove: InterVarsity, 1979), 130.

22. Fredrick C. Holmgren, "Remember Me; Remember Them," in *Scripture and Prayer*, ed. Carolyn Osiek and Donald Senior (Wilmington: Michael Glazier, 1988), 33–45.

# SELECT BIBLIOGRAPHY ON PRAYER IN THE OLD TESTAMENT

Balentine, Samuel E. *Prayer in the Hebrew Bible: The Drama of Divine-Human Dialogue.* Overtures to Biblical Theology, Minneapolis: Fortress, 1993.

Boda, Mark J., Daniel K. Falk, and Rodney A. Werline, eds. *Seeking the Favor of God: Volume I, The Origins of Penitential Prayer in Second Temple Judaism.* Early Judaism and Its Literature 21. Atlanta: SBL, 2006.

_____ *Seeking the Favor of God: Volume, II, The Development of Penitential Prayer in Second Temple Judaism.* Early Judaism and Its Literature 22. Atlanta: SBL, 2007.

_____ *Seeking the Favor of God: Volume, III, The Impact of Penitential Prayer beyond Second Temple Judaism.* Early Judaism and Its Literature 23. Atlanta: SBL, 2008.

Brueggemann, Walter. *Great Prayers of the Old Testament.* Louisville: Westminster John Knox, 2008.

Clements, Ronald E. *In Spirit and in Truth: Insights from Biblical Prayers.* Atlanta: John Knox, 1985.

Corvin, Jack W. "Stylistic and Functional Study of Prose Prayers in Historical Narratives of the Old Testament." Ph.D. diss., Emory University, 1972.

Fretheim, Terence E. *Creation Untamed: The Bible, God, and Natural Disasters.* Grand Rapids: Baker, 2010. See Chapter 5, "God, Faith, and the Practice of Prayer," pp. 123-147.

Fretheim, Terence E. "Prayer in the Old Testament: Creating Space in the World for God." Pages 51-62 in *A Primer on Prayer*. Edited by Paul R. Sponheim. Philadelphia: Fortress, 1988.

Gaiser, Frederick J. "Individual and Corporate Prayer in the Old Testament Perspective." Pages 9-22 in *A Primer on Prayer*. Edited by Paul R. Sponheim. Philadelphia: Fortress, 1988.

Goldingay, John. *Old Testament Theology: Volume Three: Israel's Life*. Downers Grove: IVP Academic, 2009. See Chapter 3, "Prayer and Thanksgiving," pp. 191-322.

Greenberg, Moshe. *Biblical Prose Prayer as a Window to the Popular Religion of Israel*. Berkeley: University of California Press, 1983. Repr., Eugene, Ore.: Wipf & Stock, 2008.

Hawkins, Ralph K. *While I Was Praying: Finding Insights about God in Old Testament Prayers*. Macon, Ga.: Smyth & Helwys, 2006.

Krinetzki, Leo. *Israels Gebet im Alten Testament*. Aschaffenburg: Paul Pattloch, 1965.

Miller, Patrick D. "Prayer and Divine Action," Pages 211-232 in *God in the Fray: A Tribute to Walter Brueggemann* eds. Tod Linafelt and Timothy K Beal; Minneapolis: Fortress, 1998.

_____ "Prayer as Persuasion: The Rhetoric and Intention of Prayer." *Word & World* 13:4 (1993): 356-362.

_____ *They Cried to the Lord: The Form and Theology of Biblical Prayer*. Minneapolis: Augsburg Fortress, 1994.

Moore, L. Paul "Prayer in the Pentateuch, Part 1" *Bibliotheca Sacra* 98:391 (1941): 329-350.

_____ "Prayer in the Pentateuch, Part 2" *Bibliotheca Sacra* 98:392 (1941): 479-488.

_____ "Prayer in the Pentateuch, Part 3" *Bibliotheca Sacra* 99:393 (1941): 108-113.

Preuss, Horst D. *Old Testament Theology*. Vol. II. Louisville: Westminster John Knox, 1992. See 13.7 "Prayer," pp. 245-250.

Reventlow, Henning G. *Gebet im Alten Testament*. Stuttgart: Kohlhammer, 1986.

Staudt, Edwin E. "Prayer and the People in the Deuteronomist." Ph.D. diss., Vanderbilt University, 1980.

Wendel, Adolf, *Das freie Laiengebet im vorexilischen Israel*. Leipzig: Eduard Pfeiffer, 1931.

Westermann, Claus. *Praise and Lament in the Psalms*. Atlanta: John Knox, 1981.

Westermann, Claus. *The Praise of God in the Psalms*. Richmond: John Knox, 1965.

# SCRIPTURE INDEX

5:8–26 | *110*
6:8–10 | *108*
7 | *108*
7:13–14 | *108*
7:15–16 | *108*
7:20–21 | *109*
7:21 | *108*
8:5 | *110*
9:28–31 | *109*
9:30–31 | *109*
9:33–34 | *110*
10 | *108*
10:3 | *108*
10:8–12 | *108*
10:12 | *108*
10:13–15 | *109*
10:18 | *108*
10:21–22 | *108*
11:13–14 | *110*
12:4b | *107*
13:20–22 | *109*
13:22 | *108*
13:23–26 | *109*
13:26–27 | *109*
14:15 | *108*
15:4b | *110*
15:12–13 | *110*
16:7 | *109*
16:7–14 | *109*
16:18–21 | *110*
16:19–21 | *110*
16:20b | *109*
19 | *109*
21 | *109*
23–24 | *109*
23:10 | *113*
26–27 | *109*
29:2–5 | *107*
30:20–21 | *109*
33:26–28 | *110*
38–39 | *112*

40:8–14 | *112*
42:1–6 | *111*
42:5 | *111*
42:7–8 | *111, 112*

**Psalms**

1 | *92, 99n6, 100n16*
1:2 | *71, 99*
1:5 | *99, 107, 113*
2 | *92, 99n5, 100n16*
2:3 | *62*
3 | *89, 99n6*
7 | *89, 99n6*
7:11 | *62*
7:14 | *62*
8:5–6 | *112*
9:4 | *64*
10:2 | *62*
11:3 | *98*
11:4 | *98*
12:4 | *62*
14 | *93, 99*
18 | *89*
18:6 | *79*
20:6–9 | *95*
23:1 | *95*
30:1 | *94*
30:2 | *94*
30:6 | *94*
34 | *89*
35:4 | *62*
35:25 | *62*
36:4 | *62*
41 | *91, 99n6*
42 | *91, 99n6*
42:7 | *80*
44:1–8 | *126*

44:11 (MT 44:12) | *62*
44:26 | *126*
48:9 | *71*
51 | *89, 99n4*
52 | *89, 99n6*
53 | *93, 99n5*
54 | *89, 99n6*
56 | *89, 99n6*
57 | *89, 99n6*
59 | *89, 99n6*
60 | *89, 99n6*
63 | *89, 99n6*
71:11 | *62*
72 | *91, 99n4*
72:20 | *91*
73 | *91, 94, 99n4*
73:1 | *95*
73:17 | *95*
73:18 | *95*
73:23 | *95*
74:2 | *126*
74:10 | *47*
74:12–17 | *126*
76 | *93, 99n6*
76:1–3 | *93*
76:4 | *93*
76:4–10 | *93*
76:7 | *93*
76:11–12 | *93*
77:7–8 | *97*
77:10–13 | *97*
77:12 | *71*
78 | *95, 99n5*
79:8–9 | *126*
79:9–10 | *126*
89 | *91, 99n6*
89:50–51 | *47*
99 | *99n6*
104:1 | *97*

104:2a | *97*
104:24 | *97*
104:34 | *97*
106 | *95, 99n6*
106:48 | *92*
111:2 | *71*
115:3 | *64*
118:5 | *79*
119:97 | *110*
120:1 | *79*
120:2 | *94*
120:3–4 | *94*
120:5–7 | *94*
126 | *90, 99n6*
132 | *91, 99n6*
132:8–10 | *155*
135:6 | *64*
136 | *95, 99n5*
137 | *90, 99n6*
137:9 | *162*
140:2 | *62*
142 | *89, 99n4*
146–150 | *92, 100*

**Proverbs**

1:1 | *103*
1:22–32 | *105*
3:5–6 | *106*
10:1 | *103*
15:8 | *103, 105*
15:29 | *105*
16:3 | *106*
18:10 | *106*
19:3 | *105*
19:23 | *106*
20:22 | *106*
21:13 | *106*
22:22–23 | *106*
23:10–11 | *106*
25:1 | *103*